The Symbolic Jesus

Historical Scholarship, Judaism and the Construction of Contemporary Identity

Religion in Culture: Studies in Social Contest and Construction

Series Editor: Russell T. McCutcheon, University of Alabama

This series is based on the assumption that those practices we commonly call religious are social practices that are inextricably embedded in various contingent, cultural worlds. Authors in this series therefore do not see the practices of religion occupying a socially or politically autonomous zone, as is the case for those who use "and" as the connector between "religion" and "culture." Rather, the range of human performances that the category "religion" identifies can be demystified by translating them into fundamentally social terms; they should therefore be seen as ways of waging the ongoing contest between groups vying for influence and dominance in intra- and inter-cultural arenas. Although not limited to one historical period, cultural site, or methodological approach, each volume exemplifies the tactical contribution to be made to the human sciences by writers who refuse to study religion as irreducibly religious; instead, each author conceptualizes religion— as well as the history of scholarship on religion—as among the various *arts de faire*, or practices of everyday life, upon which human communities routinely draw when defining and reproducing themselves in opposition to others.

Forthcoming titles in the series:

Religion and the Domestication of Dissent: Or, How to Live in a Less than Perfect Nation
Russell T. McCutcheon

It's Just Another Story: The Politics of Remembering the Earliest Christian
Willi Braun

The Symbolic Jesus

Historical Scholarship, Judaism and the Construction of Contemporary Identity

William E. Arnal

LONDON   OAKVILLE

Published by

Equinox Publishing Ltd

UK: Unit 6, The Village, 101 Amies St., London SW11 2JW

US: 28 Main Street, Oakville, CT 06779

www.equinoxpub.com

First published 2005 by Equinox Publishing Ltd.

British Library Cataloguing-in-Publication Data

A catalogue record for this book is available from the British Library.

ISBN   1-84553-006-3   (hardback)
        1-84553-007-1   (paperback)

Library of Congress Cataloging-in-Publication Data

Arnal, William E. (William Edward), 1967-
  The symbolic Jesus : historical scholarship, Judaism, and the
construction of contemporary identity / William E. Arnal.
      p. cm. -- (Religion in culture)
  Includes bibliographical references and index.
  ISBN 1-84553-006-3 (hb) -- ISBN 1-84553-007-1 (pb)
  1. Jesus Christ--Jewishness. 2. Antisemitism--History. 3. Identity
(Psychology) 4. Popular culture--North America. I. Title. II. Series.
  BT590.J8A76 2005
  232.9--dc22

                        2004016796

Typeset by ISB Typesetting, Sheffield, UK
iain@sheffieldtypesetting.com

Printed and bound in Great Britain by Antony Rowe Ltd, Chippenham, Wiltshire

Contents

Preface

The following text emerged from a public symposium hosted by the Department for the Study of Religion at the University of Toronto on March 7, 2003. The symposium, entitled, "Apocalypticism, Anti-Semitism, and the Historical Jesus: Subtexts in Criticism," was organized by Professor John S. Kloppenborg, and underwritten by the Chancellor Jackman Program for the Arts at the University of Toronto. Having been invited to produce a short paper dealing with scholarly representations of the Judaism of the historical Jesus for this symposium, I proceeded to write 129 pages on the topic, ranging from nineteenth-century anti-Semites to contemporary battles over the value of apocryphal texts, and still felt that my discussion was incomplete and under-documented. Even factoring in my own tendency to verbal excess, the issue was obviously one that could hardly be contained in an article-length paper. A short book on the subject seemed appropriate, given the wide range of issues implicated in the Judaism of Jesus, and the massive amount of scholarly output touching on this topic. I am grateful to Russell McCutcheon for inviting me to include this manuscript in his new series on "Religion in Culture: Studies in Social Contest and Construction." I could not think of a more appropriate home for this text.

I presented a vastly abbreviated version of this study at the Jackman symposium at the University of Toronto, on March 7, 2003, entitled, "How Shall we Save our Souls? The Cipher Judaism in Contemporary Historical Jesus Scholarship," and circulated an early draft of the manuscript to my fellow participants in the symposium. All of the papers presented at that symposium will be appearing as a special issue of the *Journal for the Study of the Historical Jesus*. A short version of my paper was also presented to the Saskatoon Theological Union Graduate Studies Seminar on February 13, 2004, under the title, "Subtexts in Scholarship: Historical Jesus Research and the Construction of Judaism." I wish to thank all those who have given me feedback on the addresses based on this work, and especially my fellow presenters at the Jackman symposium: Dale C. Allison, Paula Fredriksen, John S. Kloppenborg, Amy-Jill Levine, John W. Marshall, and Robert J. Miller. In addition to being first-rate scholars, these individuals are without exception also engaging and enjoyable people, and it was a pleasure to get to know them, or to get to know them better, as the case may be.

An unedited draft of the entirety of chapters 2–4 was circulated "unofficially" to a number of participants in the Society of Biblical Literature's seminar on "Ancient Myths and Modern Theories of Christian Origins," namely Ron Cameron, Barry Crawford, Burton Mack, and Merrill Miller. I wish to thank all four of them for their feedback and encouragement.

Indeed, this seminar has been my intellectual "home away from home" for the last six or seven years, and has provided an excellent forum for creative discussion of ancient Christianity, and so my appreciation extends to the entire group, whose papers and deliberations have influenced my thinking more than I would have thought possible. John S. Kloppenborg is owed particular thanks for inviting me to the conference that ultimately led to this manuscript, as are the graduate students and faculty members in the Department of Religious Studies at the University of Regina, who provide an ideal intellectual environment in which to think about and study religion. And, as always, my boundless thanks go out to Dr. Darlene Juschka—comrade-in-arms, rabble-rouser extraordinaire, indispensable intellectual influence, terrific friend.

Regina, Saskatchewan
June, 2004

1 Introduction: Mad Mel and the Cultural Prominence of Jesus

In early April of 2004, a variety of newspapers and websites carried an Associated Press story about a children's play offered by a church in Glassport, Pennsylvania. Apparently, on Saturday, April 3, the Glassport Assembly of God staged an Easter-themed performance at Glassport's memorial stadium, intended to "convey that Easter is not just about the Easter bunny, it is about Jesus Christ."[1] Pursuant to this agenda, actors in the piece whipped a performer dressed as the Easter bunny, broke Easter eggs intended for an egg hunt, and proclaimed, "there is no Easter bunny." Not everyone was appreciative: several parents complained that the event was inappropriate and distressing for their children: Melissa Salzmann's four-year old son, J.T., for instance, "was crying and asking me why the bunny was being whipped." Those who staged it, however, described the show as being a "demonstration of how Jesus was crucified."

This rationalization stands out as an exceptionally odd one in the midst of what was evidently an odd event to begin with, and deserves some attention. In what way does whipping an Easter bunny serve as a demonstration of how Jesus was crucified? What implicit and unstated assumptions are being made that link the two? No, Jesus was not crucified in a bunny suit, most historical scholars have decided, so it can't be that. And no, people did not stand around smashing Easter eggs at Golgotha either, at least according to canonical sources (though there's no telling what those Gnostics might have said). One can only conclude that the "demonstration" here revolved around the poor rabbit's flagellation. But this, too, is odd. According to all sources, Jesus died by crucifixion, a process that, as everyone knows, essentially involves attaching the body to a post, causing death by asphyxiation or exposure. Jesus was not whipped to death, and in fact the canonical Gospel accounts treat his flagellation as routine and incidental. Typical is the Gospel of Mark's terse formulation (15:15): "So Pilate, wishing to satisfy the crowd, released Barabbas for them; and after flogging Jesus, he handed him over to be crucified" (cf. Matt. 27:26b; Luke 23:16, 22, where flogging or beating is offered by Pilate as an *alternative* to crucifixion; and John 19:1). So where on earth did these people get the idea that the main player in Jesus' crucifixion was the lash?

Of course, any reader aware of current events will already know the answer to this question: the bunny's fate was sealed by Mel Gibson's movie, *The Passion of the Christ* (2004), which, among other artistic deviations from the biblical texts, offered its viewers an excruciating, extended portrayal of Jesus being flogged. There is unlikely to be any other source for this odd identification of Jesus' passion with flagellation.[2] Evidently, viewing *The Passion* inspired some Christians to insist on a return to the "real" meaning of Easter: bloodshed and torture. Prior to the movie's release, many critics feared it would inspire anti-Semitic outbursts; no one could have predicted that the real result would be an upsurge in anti-lapinism. Santa Claus had better watch his back: he might be next.

In this case, the weird excesses at the fringes of American popular culture illustrate what is true more generally: Gibson's *The Passion of the Christ*, in its bizarre equation of "spirituality" with pornographic excesses of pain, is but one symptom of the sadistically violent nature of contemporary North American culture. Commentators have tended to focus on questions of anti-Semitism, specifically, or on historical factors, the need for "historical contextualization" of the Gospel narratives, or the dangers of "literal readings" (see, e.g., Meacham 2004). But as Walter Davis observes (Davis 2004), the really striking thing about the film is precisely its unremitting and shocking use of special effects to generate two hours of violent spectacle. Davis is quite blunt about this:

> Gibson knew his film would be the hit of the season because it makes the Amerikan [*sic*] audience the offer they can't refuse: the pleasure of sado-masochistic cruelty. Piety disguises what is the true object of this film: to brutalize the audience by offering them the most extreme experience yet captured on film of the primary thing they now go to the movies for—a feast of violence. Gibson's project is to indulge in an orgy of violence masked as piety. Thereby the audience is given through their tears a way both to deny and to feel good about the sado-masochistic process needed to generate those tears. Having paid that price they get a final benefit: identification with God's rage. (Davis 2004)

All of which is, according to Davis, a function of "the condition of the American psyche: the deadening of emotion and the attempt to flee that inner state through violent acts which are needed to confer the momentary sense that one exists" (Davis 2004).

Clearly Gibson's formula was effective—pandering to prurient instinct works well; pandering to it in the guise of nobility works even better: "Evangelical congregations are buying out showings, and religious leaders are urging believers to come out in the film's opening days" (Meacham 2004, 47). Davis continues:

> Gibson's audience is crying only on the outside. Inside they have been ripened for projective identification. Their sole need is violent sado-masochistic stimuli. At film's end they have supped full with that horror and leave the feast full of rage. But with a new need—for a target on which to vent their violence. It is a mistake to confine this to the film's

patent anti-Semitism. Gibson's true achievement is the creation of a war
readiness readily transferable to Islam. (Davis 2004)

Should any reader doubt this conclusion, or think it overstated, remember
the Easter bunny. It was *precisely* as a response to this film that the strangely
and disturbingly intertwined motives of sadistic desire and religious zeal
came together in the flogging of a chocolate-bearing rabbit. The "uplifting"
violence directed against the Christ now stimulates the need to inflict
that violence on his enemies ("there is no Easter bunny"), creating a
manifest sado-masochistic confusion between the object and the subject
of violence (the bunny is whipped on Jesus' behalf, but also in imitation of
Jesus' flogging), but in both cases achieving an orgasmic (albeit short-lived)
catharsis.

It is Davis's final line, quoted above, that is perhaps most interesting.
He notes that the hatred generated by the film's intrinsic and pervasive
violence is "readily transferable to Islam." This claim is based, for the most
part, on his psychoanalytic assessment of the film's violence, which, as he
notes, generates an "identification with God's rage." At the most simple
level, this rage will be directed at whoever our enemy of the moment might
be. Given the current American and British invasions of Muslim Afghanistan
and Muslim Iraq, as well as a global "war on (Muslim) terrorism" by the
United States, the target is obvious, all the more so when the most intuitive
contrast to one religious tradition will be another: Islam versus Christianity.
More than this, the movie invites us to identify as the "natural" targets of
(our) divine rage those who perpetrated the unasked-for violence against
the innocent victim. While in the movie, those perpetrators were "the Jews"
(for the most part), the structural equivalent to this in the reality of most
viewers will be the hijackers of 9/11 who attacked an "innocent" America
(see Mack 1988) struck dumb by the unasked-for horror of "senseless"
hatred and violence.

But one can, and should, go even further than Davis on this point. The
tropes of prejudice are easily transferable: for "Western" audiences, the dark
skin, hooked noses, and inscrutable "other-ness" of the Jew of anti-Semitic
propaganda (including Gibson's film) signifies the contemporary Arab more
easily and directly than it does the contemporary Jew. Few people these
days believe such slanders as the claim that Jews control the banks; but very
many believe that Arabs, more or less indiscriminately, are terrorists. Few
accept the factuality of the ridiculous conspiracies of the *Protocols of the
Elders of Zion* (although there are always nutters who will believe anything),
or much care one way or another; but as of January 2003, 44 percent of
Americans believed that some or most of the hijackers who flew into the
World Trade towers and the Pentagon in September 2001 were Iraqis, in
spite of the *fact* that none of them were. Racist hatred and fear of the "other"
has been redirected in our own time from the Jews—who are no longer an

"acceptable" target and who are, at least in North America and western Europe, not especially "other" anymore—to the Arabs, alternately presented as contemptible and ridiculous (e.g., in the 1999 film, *The Mummy*), or as malevolent and treacherous (especially since September 11th 2001). Ironically, anti-*Semitism*, strictly and literally speaking, is still alive and well, but its target has shifted from one group of Semites to another.[3] The torture of Arab prisoners by American forces at Iraq's Abu Ghraib prison, many of them arrested by mistake and guilty of no crime at all, reveals a racist attitude wholly akin to that of Nazi camp guards: these people are sub-human. No, I am not claiming that the relatively restricted incidence of torture and war crimes in Iraq is comparable to the Holocaust, nor do I believe that Americans in general are interested in enacting a genocide against the world's Arab population. But what I am claiming is that the attitudes that *allowed* the Holocaust to happen are shared today by many Americans: the *Untermenschen* (whoever they may be) have no rights that the Master Race need recognize. The details associated with the Abu Ghraib scandal will be familiar to anyone even remotely conscious of the Nazi regime: the indiscriminate identification of victims; the gleeful enjoyment of now-unfettered sadism; the proudly-posed photographs; the piles of naked bodies; even the excuses of the soldiers who were "just following orders."

This chain of connections between beaten bunnies, a movie about Jesus, contemporary anti-Semitism, anti-Arab sentiment, and the invasion of Iraq—extended and perhaps tenuous though it be—illustrates, if anything, just how complex and multi-faceted cultural symbolism is, and how indirect and unstable the cultural *work* done by symbols can be. We may be certain that Gibson himself did not intend to produce a movie that would lead to unprovoked attacks on the Easter bunny. Yet this seems to have been one consequence. To my mind there is little question that there *was* an intention to manipulate the audience's rage and to co-ordinate it with the film's cathartic sadism; but the targets of that rage were not so easily directed, whatever Gibson's wishes may have been. Pre-release predictions of anti-Semitic violence and other outbursts made perfect sense in light of the content of the movie, as well as the dismal history of Christian reactions to the "passion play," of which this movie is simply the most recent, and spectacular, avatar. But these resoundingly logical and sensible predictions did not appear, for the most part, to come to pass. In fact, the organization B'nai Brith Canada announced in April of 2004 that anti-Semitic incidents increased in 2003, that is, considerably *before* Gibson's *Passion* was released (CBC 2004a).

The exception proves the rule: the most egregious incidence of anti-Jewish violence to take place in Canada, at least, immediately after the release of *The Passion*, was the vandalism of the United Talmud Torah elementary school in Montreal, in which the school library was deliberately set on fire and destroyed (CBC 2004a). Those whom the police arrested and charged with the crime, however, turned out not to be *Christians*, spurred on by Gibson's murderous vision of Jesus' death, but *Muslims*, and in fact a note left at the scene of the crime indicated that the vandalism was an act of retaliation for Israel's assassination of Hamas leader Sheik Ahmed Yassin (CBC 2004b). Moreover, the reaction to this crime by the predominantly Christian population and leadership of Canada was most decidedly neither satisfaction nor indifference but outrage and horror. As Michael Neumann argues, Canadians seem to express disproportionately *greater* indignation at anti-Semitic actions than at hate crimes directed against any other identifiable entity (Neumann 2004). And so immediately after the release of *The Passion*, the most notable anti-Semitic act to take place in Canada was apparently perpetrated by non-Christians, and led to an outburst of *anti*-anti-Semitism.

And so it would appear that the effects of cultural symbolism, the actual work symbols do as they are received and appropriated, is often indirect and non-linear. Like light or sound, cultural symbolism will be bent and distorted by the medium through which it must pass: the prevailing concerns, assumptions, and prejudices of those who receive it. If the communication, in its original form or intent, fails completely to conform to the experiences and beliefs of those to whom it is directed, it will not—cannot—be heeded. In North America, especially among intellectuals, media and political figures, and the well-educated in general, anti-Semites are about as popular as pedophiles or compulsive nose-pickers. Thus the effect, the actual cultural work done, of a movie such as *The Passion of the Christ*, whether its anti-Judaism or anti-Semitism is deliberate or merely incidental, has shifted and bent. It failed to deliver its anti-Jewish payload, at least in North America, almost inevitably. The movie's violence, sadism, and righteousness were successfully communicated, however, but the target of those sentiments, represented by "the Jews" in the movie, has been directed elsewhere, at times ridiculously.

The thesis of the following pages is that scholarship on the historical Jesus uses the figure of Jesus as a screen or symbol on which to project contemporary cultural debates, and to employ the inherent authority of this Jesus-figure to advance one or another particular stance on these debates. This is especially true, I argue, for issues and polemics concerning the Jewish identity and religiosity of Jesus. As with Gibson's movie, the image of a Jewish Jesus is both contentious, and, I argue, symbolic beyond its literal parameters. In fact, no one in mainstream New Testament scholarship denies that Jesus was a Jew, and so the acrimony connected to this issue seems to be generated by other, implicit or hidden concerns, which the issue of Jesus' Judaism is somehow, obliquely, communicating. And also as with Gibson's movie, these symbolic significances may have very little to do with the explicit intentions of the participants in the debate, and much more to do with the *reception* of the scholarly literature.

Chapter 2 endeavors to sketch out, albeit briefly, the tropes and attitudes behind some of the genuinely anti-Semitic scholarship on Jesus of the nineteenth and early twentieth centuries, and to introduce accusations of scholarly anti-Jewish sentiments in *contemporary* work on the historical Jesus, which, according to some charges, has produced reconstructions of a Jesus who is not Jewish at all. In chapter 3, I argue that these accusations are irresponsible and badly misplaced. On the one hand, the scholars who normally are targets of such criticisms are neither anti-Jewish in their own agendas, nor do they, in fact, produce images of Jesus that are somehow non-Jewish. And on the other hand, those scholars who make these accusations seem to be relying on a particularly rigid and reified definition of Judaism—a characterization that cannot be sustained. In chapter 4, I attempt to explain why it is that so much energy and rancor are expended in this debate over what is essentially a non-issue. I argue here that, since in fact all parties to the "debate" actually agree on the point being debated—that Jesus was Jewish—the discussion must be fueled by something else, which Jesus' Judaism is being used to symbolize. I attempt to identify this symbolic freight as consisting of issues of *identity* and self-definition: scholarly, political, religious, and cultural. Finally, chapter 5 aims at some inconclusive conclusions.

The substantial chapters of this book (chapters 2, 3, and 4) were already written by March of 2003, well before Gibson's movie was released, and in fact before I had even heard of the plans for it. When I did finally hear about it, and witnessed the controversy it generated even before its release, I was forced to concede that my conclusions here were, if anything, understated. *The Passion* was arguably anti-Jewish; but it was *unarguably* controversial. Articles appeared criticizing the film before it had even been seen (e.g., Fredriksen 2003). *Newsweek* magazine offered a cover story on the film, again, prior to its release (Meacham 2004). Websites devoted space to enumerating the various departures of the movie from its biblical sources (www.beliefnet.com). And the largest proportion of this extensive commentary was concerned, not with the usual question of whether this was an entertaining, engaging movie, but with questions of the film's "historical" accuracy, its theological implications, its likelihood to have (or not to have) deleterious effects. An earlier Gibson effort, *Braveheart* (1995), similarly bloody, righteous, and unhistorical, elicited no similar controversy, nor did anyone predict that its unappealing representation of the English occupation of Scotland would result in anti-English hate crimes. Jesus, however, and especially the representation of Jesus' relations with other Jews, is an entirely different matter.

Gibson's movie, and especially the reaction to it, thus does teach us at least two things worth knowing about Jesus. The first is that he is an extraordinarily important, and contested, cultural symbol, as my analysis of historical Jesus scholarship assumes. Gibson convinced me that my basic assumption was right: Jesus means so much, so differently, to so many people, that it is almost impossible to say anything about him without engaging people's most deeply-cherished feelings—about right and wrong, about who "we" are, about the meaning of our behaviors and principles. Whether it is a scholarly study of the historical Jesus or a cinematic representation of the Christ of the gospels, any and all treatments will necessarily speak to any and all of the connections between Jesus in the popular (and scholarly) imagination and those aspects of life and meaning that this Jesus informs. A statement about Jesus, it would seem, is always a statement about something else, controversial, rich with implications.

The second lesson Mel has to teach us is that the *scholarly* debate about this cultural symbol is much less relevant and influential than we would like to think. Scholars, and the people who read their work, are no different than others: they have the same kinds of concerns, beliefs, and assumptions about the world they live in. And so scholarly discourse on Jesus will tend to reveal the same kinds of concerns that animate the more popular conversations about Jesus, to which the controversy around Gibson's *Passion* attests. On the one side of that controversy were the various articles and statements that were critical—for good reason—of the movie. But on the other side were all those *millions* who, either ignoring or even in adverse reaction to the pre-release critiques, voted with their feet and paid to see the movie, at least in part as an emphatic defense of Christianity itself in the face of modern skepticism and "liberal intellectuals." We scholars, in our conversations about Jesus, tend to ignore or dismiss the vast majority of the public, who return the favor and show little or no interest in or even cognizance of our discourses. Jesus is indeed a valuable cultural commodity. It turns out, though, that if the sheer weight of numbers means anything at all, the rarefied opinions of scholars—to which this book is devoted—contribute almost nothing to the public conversation about the symbolic Jesus.

2 Bad Karma: Anti-Semitism in New Testament Scholarship

In 1899, Houston Stewart Chamberlain published his massive *Foundations of the Nineteenth Century* (Chamberlain 1977), hundreds of pages purporting to track and explain both the triumphs and tragedies of Europe of the 1800s. The focus of his discussion was mainly cultural: the artistic high points and pedestrian low points of European civilization were laid bare by reference to history, cultural influences of various sorts, and the natural playing out of tendencies inherent in this or that aspect of the peoples in question. The tome was hugely popular and hugely influential (so Davies 1975, 575).

In the course of his treatment, Chamberlain was required to address and evaluate the vicissitudes of Christian influence on European culture. Central to this analysis was the pressing question of the relation in which Jesus stood to Judaism, and indeed, whether or not he was himself Jewish:

> Let us therefore ask ourselves, was Christ a Jew by race? The question seems at the first glance somewhat childish. In the presence of such a personality peculiarities of race shrink to nothingness. An Isaiah, however much he may tower above his contemporaries, remains a thorough Jew; not a word did he utter that did not spring from the history and spirit of his people; even when he mercilessly exposes and condemns what is characteristically Jewish, he proves himself—especially in this—the Jew. (Chamberlain 1977, 1:201)

Chamberlain claims that the question is complicated by two key factors. The first is that there is a difference between being a Jew by religion, and being a Jew by race (1977, 1:202). Chamberlain reserves his deepest scorn for those scholars who allege that Jesus' religious identity is more important, historically, than his racial identity. Referring to the French comparativist Albert Réville, who dismissed the question of whether Jesus was an Aryan on the grounds that what was important was the nation in which Jesus was raised, i.e., his culture, Chamberlain laments:

> This is what people called "science" in the year of grace 1896! To think that at the close of the nineteenth century a professor could still be ignorant that the form of the head and the structure of the brain exercise quite distinctive influence upon the form and structure of the thoughts, so that the influence of the surroundings, however great it may be estimated to be, is yet by this initial fact of the physical tendencies confined to definite capacities and possibilities, in other words, has definite paths marked out for it to follow! To think that he could fail to know that the shape of the skull in particular is one

of those characteristics which are inherited with ineradicable persistency, so that races are distinguished by craniological measurements, and, in the case of mixed races, the original elements which occur by atavism become still manifest to the investigator! ... O Middle Ages! when will your night leave us? (1977, 1:210)

The second complication is that Israelites of the northern Levant, particularly Galilee, are racially distinct from the "real Jews" of Judea in the south; indeed, the former may include an influx of folks with "purely Aryan blood" (Chamberlain 1977, 1:203 n.† and 205–7). As it happens, Chamberlain concludes, the history and ethnic compositions of Galilee make it unlikely—indeed, nearly impossible—for Jesus himself to have been a Jew by race. Among arguments based on the historical relations of Galileans with Judeans, and of both with the Gentile world around them, Chamberlain also contends that, "There are many reports too of the special beauty of the women of Galilee; moreover, the Christians of the first centuries speak of their great kindness, and contrast their friendliness with the haughty contemptuous treatment they met with at the hands of genuine Jewesses" (Chamberlain 1977, 1:208). He further argues that the dialect of Galilean Aramaic was distinctive in its improper pronunciation of gutturals, asserting that, "This fact points to a physical difference in the form of the larynx and would alone lead us to suppose that a strong admixture of non-Semitic blood had taken place; for the profusion of gutturals and facility in using them are features common to all Semites" (Chamberlain 1977, 1:209). On the basis of such considerations as these, as well as the unique genius of Jesus' own message, Chamberlain finally surmises that:

> Whoever makes the assertion that Christ was a Jew is either ignorant or insincere: ignorant when he confuses religion and race, insincere when he knows the history of Galilee and partly conceals, partly distorts the very entangled facts in favor of his religious prejudices or, it may be, to curry favor with the Jews. The probability that Christ was no Jew, that He had not a drop of genuinely Jewish blood in his veins, is so great that it is almost equivalent to a certainty ... His advent is not the perfecting of the Jewish religion but its negation ... [T]he feelings are ... the fountain head of all genuine religion; this spring which the Jews had well-nigh choked with their formalism and hard-hearted rationalism Christ opened up. (Chamberlain 1977, 1:211–12, 221)

In short, then, Chamberlain explains that the greatness of the Christian message owes nothing to Judaism, or, indeed, to individuals tainted by Jewish ethnicity. Jesus himself, if not an Aryan, was at least no Jew. European culture, even in its Christian-influenced elements, was safe from contamination by Jewish thought-processes.

Chamberlain, while an excellent example of the kinds of ideas assumed and promoted by nineteenth-century racist scholarship, as well as of their vacuity, was neither the first nor the last intellectual to put considerable effort into distancing the historical figure of Jesus either from the religious ideology of Judaism, or from "racial" affiliation with Judaism, or both. Probably the most well-known example of both tendencies in twentieth-century New Testament scholarship is found in the work of Walter Grundmann, whose arguments were very similar to those laid down by Chamberlain (see especially Grundmann 1940). Jesus, Grundmann claimed, was a Jew neither by heart nor by blood. The fundamental opposition of Jesus' teachings to Judaism can be illustrated historically, by showing the roots of Jesus' thought in non-Jewish influences, and, more graphically, by pointing to the fact of Jesus' crucifixion by "the Jews," as sure an indication as any of the antipathy of Judaism to the gospel message (see Johnson 1986, 9–10). In addition, Grundmann rehearsed in a rather more informed fashion than Chamberlain[1] the arguments about the ethnic composition of Galilee, pointing to such phenomena as the minimal penetration of Galilee during the monarchic period, the Assyrian deportation, the presence of Greek papyri as early as the third century BCE, the Hasmonean removal of Jews from Galilee, the later necessity of forcible conversion of the Galilean population by John Hyrcanus, and finally Herod's settling of German [!] cavalry there (Grundmann 1940, 169–75; cf. Johnson 1986, 10–11; Heschel 1994, 597). Grundmann concluded, predictably enough, that in light of Jesus' anti-Jewish message, combined with the historical anthropology of Galilee, it would be unwise to conclude that Jesus was a Jew in the "völkisch" sense (Grundmann 1940, 175; cf. Johnson 1986, 11).

Grundmann's agenda, like Chamberlain's, clearly was motivated not simply by an anti-Jewish animus, but by a genuinely anti-Semitic ideology. In Grundmann's case, too, the matter intersected directly with the political sphere: like many other New Testament scholars living under a Nazi government,[2] Grundmann—a member of the Nazi party since 1930 (Heschel 1994, 592), *before* Hitler's rise to power—devoted his historical scholarship to buttressing anti-Semitic (and genocidal) Nazi assumptions and policies. In the process, he also attempted to ensure the relevance of his own area of study and his own theological commitment to Christianity in an environment in which Christianity fell under suspicion as a non-Aryan religious tradition. From May of 1939 he served as academic director of the "Institute for the Study and Eradication of Jewish Influence on the Church Life of the German Volk" (Heschel 1994, 591). Susannah Heschel draws particular attention to the ways in which the Nazification of New Testament studies and Christianity in general was not simply ideological assimilation, but also a defensive effort at survival in a Nazi environment: "The problem Grundmann faced was answering Nazi accusations that because Christians worshipped a Jewish God, they had no place in the National Socialist state" (Heschel 1994, 597; cf. Grundmann 1940, 1).

It is not especially difficult to condemn overt Nazism and its ideology. But it should be stressed that the matter of Christian *and* scholarly complicity with Nazi anti-Semitism and thus, directly or indirectly, with the Holocaust, does not begin or end with Grundmann. Nazi anti-Semitism itself did not arise in a vacuum, but represented a continuation of racialist anti-Semitism popularized and given pseudo-scientific legitimacy in the nineteenth century by writers such as Chamberlain. But this anti-Semitism—not so much in its choice of motifs, accusations, and rationales, as in its choice of a favorite scapegoat—ultimately finds its parentage in Christian anti-Judaism, which extends from the New Testament period right up to modernity, and which set the tone for the exclusion of European Jews from the "blood and soil" romanticizing (and then intellectualizing) of national identity in the nineteenth century.

This ultimately Christian lineage is exemplified in the "humane" anti-Semitism of Gerhard Kittel, the original editor of the *Theologisches Wörterbuch zum Neuen Testament* (English translation, *TDNT* [Kittel 1964–76]), a collaborator with Grundmann, and an outspoken purveyor of anti-Judaism during the Nazi period. Kittel directly addressed himself to "the Jewish Question" in a 1933 book of the same title, *Die Judenfrage*. On the one hand, he argued that any solution to "the Jewish Question" be legal, avoid barbaric methods, and in fact retain a place in Germany for Jews (Johnson 1986, 16–18). Christians must remember that Jesus himself was a Jew (contra Chamberlain, Grundmann, *et al.*), and that the Jews were (once) God's chosen people. Indeed, Kittel says, Christians have as much an obligation to preach the gospel to Jews, to try to convert them, as to any other people. *However*, "the only sensible and tolerable form of Judaism is that in which the Jews remain in the position of nonassimilated guests" (Kittel, *Judenfrage*, 40, quoted in Johnson 1986, 17): they should not be granted citizenship or equal rights, and they should not be allowed to influence the dominant culture (Ericksen 1999, 34–35). Why such separation and discrimination? Because it is a reflection of God's judgement on disobedient Israel. In particular, "from the 'Christian point of view' this people became homeless because they crucified the one who was the fulfillment of their divine history" (Johnson 1986, 18, quoting Kittel, *Judenfrage*).

What is especially notable about this argument is what it lacks: it does not call for the extermination of the Jewish people, and it does not seem to appeal to the "scientific" racialist theories of physiological Jewish inferiority which characterize genuine anti-*Semitism*. And yet, in a context in which anti-Semitism had been elevated to one of *the* key issues in German politics, Kittel offers arguments for the necessity of punishing "the Jews" and links these explicitly to the Christian message. Even if Kittel's views are properly seen as theological (and distinctively Christian) anti-Judaism, rather than as anti-Semitism, he shows how the former can be actively complicit in the latter, and thus also actively complicit in genocide. He also provides an illustration of how theological anti-Judaism can shade over into genuine racial anti-Semitism, as some of his later works attempt to develop theories that a "mongrelized" exilic Jewish "race" has historically been driven by a desire for world domination and marked by sexually perverse behaviors toward "Aryan" women (see Ericksen 1999, 35–36).

Perhaps even more striking is the "business as usual" New Testament scholarship carried out during the Nazi era (so also Johnson 1986, 19). Between the extremes of resistance to and endorsement of Nazi anti-Semitism were the less-visible but more common instances of German scholars seemingly unaffected by the Nazi government. These include, among other, Ernst Lohmeyer, Martin Dibelius, Ernst Käsemann, Werner Georg Kümmel, Oscar Cullmann, and Rudolph Bultmann (Johnson 1986, 19). It would be inappropriate, in the absence of direct evidence, to characterize scholars such as these as anti-Semites. And yet living under a massively and actively anti-Semitic government did not, apparently, have much of an impact on their research. To my mind, this suggests a *congruence* of sorts between the historical and religious assumptions of such scholars and the active anti-Semitic agenda of the Nazi state. Without speculating on the private opinions of these scholars, one may still surmise that their scholarly activities reflected views that, at the very least, were not regarded as inimical to Nazi ideology. As Kittel's position indicates, at least part of this congruence may rest with theological anti-Judaism, stemming from the polemical writings of the New Testament, and from the Christian conviction that "the Jews" both rejected the gospel and killed the son of God.

But there is more. The scholarly analysis of both the historical Jesus and the character of the earliest church, at least as undertaken by theologically sophisticated *Christians* (as has normally been the case), has tended to have an apologetic dimension; such critical scholarship has often aimed, overtly or covertly, to demonstrate the validity of the Christian gospel. And, more often than not, one of the key pillars in such a demonstration is the claim that Jesus and his first followers were in some critical fashion *distinctive, unique.*[3] This theological conviction of the uniqueness of Christianity as exemplified in its founder—by no means an intrinsically anti-Jewish sentiment—is typically manifested in historical scholarship via a *contrast* between Jesus and his environment. Were that environment medieval Scandinavia,[4] then the *genius* of Jesus would be illustrated by its contrast to the views of his Norse and Finnish contemporaries, and we would be treated to an exposition on the limitations of Norse modes of thought, or of Finnish religiosity. As it happens, of course, Jesus' actual historical environment was first-century Palestine; his contemporaries and interlocutors, mainly Jews. And so at least Christian historical scholarship on Jesus and the gospels has, predictably, in the interests of Jesus' unique genius, tended to emphasize the *contrast* between him and his environment.

This contrast is present even in those scholarly works that post-date the Holocaust, and that were written by academics who show little evidence of being anti-Semitic. It often entails some form of serious distortion, either by constructing a portrait of Jesus that is little more than wish-fulfillment, or by characterizing "Judaism" in such a rigid and prejudicial way that it becomes much easier for nearly *any* well-rounded historical figure to "transcend" it. This practice of rendering Judaism in crude strokes in order to enhance the comparative "genius" of Jesus is as old as Renan's *Life of Jesus* (see Baird 1992, 1:379). Renan describes the Pharisees as "men of narrow mind, caring much for externals; their devoutness was haughty, formal, and self-satisfied. Their manners were ridiculous, and excited the smiles of even those who respected them…. This strictness [in legal observance] was, in fact, often only apparent, and concealed in reality great moral laxity" (Renan 1935 [1863], 170).[5] But much later, Bultmann, while insisting that "Jesus stands in the historical context of Jewish expectations about the end of the world and God's new future" (Bultmann 1951, 1:4), nonetheless returns to the tired old motif of Jesus' message as a reaction to and condemnation of Judaism:

> As interpretation of the will, the demand, of God, Jesus' message is a great *protest against Jewish legalism*—i.e., against a form of piety which regards the will of God as expressed in the written Law and in the Tradition which interprets it, a piety which endeavors to win God's favor by the toil of minutely fulfilling the Law's stipulations…. The result is not merely that a mass of ordinances which have lost the meaning they once had under earlier conditions remains in force and so have to be twisted by artificial interpretation into relevance for today; not merely that regulations appropriate to the present have to be wrung out of the ancient Law by artificial deduction to meet the new conditions of life … The real result is that motivation to ethical conduct is vitiated. (Bultmann 1951, 1:11; emphasis original)

Presumably, it is not necessary to cite the massive and compelling scholarly literature refuting the characterization of Second Temple Jewish religiosity as "legalistic" in the sense here offered by Bultmann, or, for that matter, Renan.

One turns to the scholarship of Bultmann's contemporaries and to the following "new quest" for the historical Jesus only to find, again and again, the same basic constellation of ideas. Käsemann offers a particularly sharp expression of this sensibility:

> To this [teaching of the historical Jesus] there are no Jewish parallels, nor indeed can there be. For the Jew who does what is done here has cut himself off from the community of Judaism—or else he brings the

Messianic Torah and is therefore the Messiah ... while Jesus may have made his appearance in the first place in the character of a rabbi or a prophet, nevertheless his claim far surpasses that of any rabbi or prophet ... he cannot be integrated into the background of the Jewish piety of his time. Certainly he was a Jew and made the assumptions of Jewish piety, but at the same time he shatters this framework with his claim. (Käsemann 1964, 37–38)

One can find similar passages simply by examining New Testament scholarship from the 1950s, 1960s, and even into the 1970s, more or less at random. So, for instance, Joachim Jeremias (1965, 21):

We are now in a position to say why abba is not used in Jewish prayers as an address to God: to a Jewish mind, it would have been irreverent and therefore unthinkable to call God by this familiar word. It was therefore new, something unique and unheard of, that Jesus dared to take this step and speak with God as a child speaks with his father, simply, intimately, securely.

Norman Perrin and Dennis C. Duling, in a popular New Testament introduction, assert that, "... Jesus challenged the tendency of the Jewish community of his day to fragment itself and in the name of God to reject certain of its own members. This aroused a deep-rooted opposition to him ..." (Perrin and Duling 1982, 412). C. K. Barrett puts the matter in especially bald terms:

The far more important theological issue lay between Jesus and the Jews. It was not the question whether Jesus did or did not fill certain recognized Jewish positions, such as that of the Messiah; it was the question whether grace or legalism represented the truth about God, whether true and final dominion belonged to the Torah or to the Son of man. (Barrett 1968, 67)

He adds a somewhat conciliatory note at the end of this passage: "It is not suggested that Judaism is intrinsically legalistic, still less that Christian thought has never been corrupted by legalism. But there certainly was a marked legalistic development in first-century Judaism which went far beyond mere faithfulness to Torah, and it was against this that Jesus (and Paul) reacted ..." (Barrett 1968, 67 n.48).

I would contend, however, that none of this more recent scholarship is motivated by anti-Semitic, or even theologically anti-Jewish, convictions held personally by the scholars in question. The problem is much larger and more insidious than this. What contrasts between Jesus and Judaism such as these indicate is the way in which insistence on Jesus' uniqueness and transcendence (necessarily?) implies at least a sharp opposition between Jesus and his religious, social, or cultural context, which happens, of course, to be Jewish (so also Davies 1975, 569); and at worst this opposition or contrast degenerates into outright denigration of that (Jewish) context. It is true that, historically, the Christian Gospel has carried with it the seeds of anti-Judaism in its story of a god allegedly killed by the very people he was sent to save. But even among the most good-willed Christians, who may reject that particular reading of the Christian myth, there is still the necessity to assert Jesus' distinctiveness. And with this necessity comes, logically, a need to emphasize the extent to which Jesus was not ordinary; hence, not an ordinary Jew.

The absence of a hateful intent behind such reasoning does not, I think, absolve its purveyors. A willingness to distort and denigrate the religious beliefs of an entire people—and in particular an *ethnos* which since the Middle Ages has at best been ghettoized and at worst subjected to pogroms and deliberate genocide—betrays, in addition to its scholarly deficiencies, a moral bankruptcy that cannot be rationalized. The karmic stain thus engendered by Christianity (which, after all, appears to have invented racial anti-Semitism in Medieval Spain [so Davies 1975]) and by scholars of ancient Christianity is not the sort of thing to be purged in a generation or two. Certainly, Christians "forgiving" "the Jews" for killing Christ will not suffice, nor will limp assertions that the deicides of yesterday are not the same individuals as the Jews of today. For Christianity to transcend its hateful legacy will require not only a distancing from the kinds of thinking that contributed to this outrage; but also a sustained demonstration over a long period of time that Christianity can abstain from *any* forms of either racism or xenophobia; and a sustained demonstration of scholarship that is actually scholarship, and not wish-fulfillment. My hopes are not high. Others, however, are more optimistic:

> The conclusions historians draw remain at best highly educated conjectures. Moreover, even if we could firmly conclude that the evangelists and their audiences did not have anti-Jewish views, the fact remains that throughout the subsequent centuries, later Christians have often interpreted the texts in this manner. Divorced from any historical context, many of the passages in the Gospels and Acts remain a challenge for those who would seek to improve Jewish-Christian relations. There is much in the New Testament that the vast majority of contemporary Christians no longer take literally.... Through history, through what some would call the actions of the Holy Spirit, texts that negate the fullness of human life, texts that appear to enjoin evil, slavery, or war, are given new interpretations. The time is surely here for the anti-Jewish texts, or, perhaps put better, the texts that can and have been seen as anti-Jewish, to undergo the same critical, merciful treatment. (Levine 2002, 98)

However, in the case of critical scholarship on the New Testament, earliest Christianity, and especially the historical Jesus, things have been improving for the last thirty years or so. Beginning in the 1970s and continuing to the present, numerous studies of the historical Jesus have appeared which not only acknowledge his identity as a Jew, but which emphasize it, and make it central to their reconstructions. Even the titles of such works reflect a contrast with earlier reconstructions: *Jesus the Jew* (Vermès 1973), *Jesus and Judaism* (Sanders 1985), *A Marginal Jew* (Meier 1991), *The Historical Jesus: The Life of a Mediterranean Jewish Peasant* (Crossan 1991), *The Religion of Jesus the Jew* (Vermès 1993), *Jesus of Nazareth, King of the Jews: A Jewish Life and the Emergence of Christianity* (Fredriksen 1999), and others. To some degree, I have to attribute this shift in sensibilities to the fact that over the last few decades New Testament and historical Jesus scholarship has, at least overtly, become less and less theologically oriented. There is, therefore, less and less of a concern with the uniqueness and transcendence of Jesus, and correspondingly greater concern with situating him within a sensible historical environment that at least in part accounts—not merely serves as a setting—for his activity. Thus is it a normal feature of the recent works emphasizing Jesus' Judaism that they tend to *normalize* him, make him an understandable and more ordinary figure among his contemporaries, comparable to other Jewish figures from the same time and place. This is equally true of a great deal of recent scholarship that does *not* place central emphasis on Jesus' Judaism, but focuses its comparative analysis on specifically Galilean social and cultural life, or which widens the focus to include the whole Mediterranean world. In either case, we are beginning to learn how to deal with a genuinely *historical* Jesus, a figure who is a *part* of his world (however that world be conceptualized), rather than a radiant *exception* to it.

Strangely, however, the insistence on the Jewishness of Jesus has become, in the last decade or so, increasingly shrill, dogmatic, and polemical. In the 1970s and 1980s, the inclusion of the words "Jew" or "Judaism" in the title of a book on Jesus was a refreshing rejoinder to the scholarship of previous decades. By the 1990s and into the third millennium, it seemed that one could hardly write about Jesus at all without actively asserting his Jewish roots somehow in the title of the book or article. One is left with the sense that there is a marked defensive intention behind such wording, that Jesus' Judaism needs to be protected strenuously. The corrective focus we see in titles of works of Sanders and Vermès made sense at the time; the abundance of similar titles some twenty or more years later is rather odd. Even more striking has been the proliferation of charges that certain *contemporary* reconstructions of the historical Jesus are un-Jewish or even—it is implied—anti-Jewish. A surprising number of recent scholars have articulated a *need* to safeguard the Jewishness of Jesus. Seán Freyne, for instance, in a rejoinder to Crossan's work, has claimed recently that:

> To water down the Jewishness of Galilee not only has the potential for anti-Semitism, as Walter Grundmann's 1941 book on Jesus the Galilean shows, it also involves a refusal to acknowledge that the Christian understanding of God is also grounded in the Jewish religious experience. (Freyne 1997, 91)[6]

A more direct indication of why the Judaism of Jesus might require defense has been offered by N. T. Wright, with particular (and woefully inaccurate[7]) reference to scholarship on Q. The majority of Q scholars, he asserts, argue that:

> Q reflects a very early Christian community for whom the Jewish stories, both in form and content, were not particularly important. The focus, instead, was on a different style and content of teaching: the Hellenistic philosophy known as Cynicism, on the one hand, and, on the other, a tradition of teaching which offered a secret wisdom, a secret Gnosis. It was, in fact, a community that would have been just as happy with the Gospel of Thomas. Jesus was a teacher of aphoristic, quasi-Gnostic, quasi-Cynic wisdom. (Wright 1992, 437)

Such a reconstruction, of course, is rejected by Wright. A similar, if more vitriolic and intemperate, characterization is offered by Birger Pearson, this time of the Jesus Seminar:

> The Jesus of the Jesus Seminar is a non-Jewish Jesus. To put it metaphorically, the Seminar has performed a forcible epispasm on the historical Jesus, a surgical procedure for removing the marks of circumcision. The result might arouse some disquiet in the minds of people who know the history of the 30's and 40's of our century. But the Jesus of the Jesus Seminar is much too banal to cause us to think that the ideology producing him is like that which produced the "Aryan Jesus" of the 1930's. (Pearson 1996, 42)

Accusations and defensive reactions of this sort are especially marked in rejoinders to the so-called "Cynic hypothesis"—the claim that the historical Jesus might be illuminated by comparison to ancient Cynic philosophers.[8] Over against this approach, one again and again encounters the claim that instead of being comparable to the Cynics, Jesus is, rather, *Jewish*. For instance, referring to Burton Mack's descriptions of Jesus as Cynic-like in *A Myth of Innocence* (Mack 1988), Hans Dieter Betz complains that "revising Jesus' 'social role in Galilee' removes Jesus, on the one hand, from the Jewish role of eschatological prophet, and, on the other hand, from loyalty toward Jerusalem" (Betz 1994, 457). Paul Rhodes Eddy, similarly, asserts that "the Cynic model of sage becomes highly questionable with regard to Jesus. Instead, it is the model of *Jewish sage* that offers the most apparent parallel.... [O]ne of the most characteristic forms of Jesus' teaching style— the parable—has no real Cynic parallels and is a fundamentally *Jewish* form" (Eddy 1996, 460–61; emphasis original).

Perhaps the strangest and most embarrassing of this recent string of accusations and insinuations is E. P. Sanders's recent article speculating on the motives of those scholars who, purportedly, construct a non-Jewish Jesus (Sanders 2002). Sanders raises the specter of an anti-Jewish agenda in his description of the procedures behind (most) historical Jesus research:

> What is common to all the questers, whether early or recent, is the view that some of the material in the Gospels is "authentic" and represents the real historical Jesus, who should be followed, while other material should be rejected … Not infrequently, the parts of the Gospels that some people regard as silly and obviously bad, and which they wish not to attribute to Jesus, come from ancient Judaism. This gives an anti-Jewish bias to the separation of wheat from chaff. (Sanders 2002, 34)

But then Sanders dismisses personally-held anti-Judaism as an unlikely motivation among such scholars, and opines instead that the real problem is that modern scholars dislike ancient culture in general:

> It is an odd fact, but many of the people whose interests take them into the study of the ancient world dislike it. In the case of many New Testament scholars, the only parts of the ancient world of which they have knowledge are those parts that crop up in the New Testament. In the study of Jesus, the ancient world that they encounter is Jewish. Since some of these scholars want to distance Jesus from his ancient environment, they often attack and denigrate Judaism, but in many cases what they actually dislike is the ancient world, and they simply attack the version of it that they meet in the Gospels. Their hearts, in other words, may be perfectly free of dislike of the Jewish people … (Sanders 2002, 34–35)

The portrayal of Jesus in recent scholarship in such ways that, supposedly, vitiate or minimize his Jewishness is simply bad scholarship, stemming from a desire to portray Jesus in attractive ways, and seeing the most typical features of antique religiosity—sacrifice, purity issues, etc.—as unattractive. Sanders does not, however, provide any actual *examples* of these supposed tendencies. Interestingly, he characterizes the critical procedures of sifting core historical material from later embellishments *solely* in terms of the motivation of congeniality, and asserts that *all* questers after the historical Jesus believe that he is a normative figure, that he should be followed.

Between the repeated and defensive insistence on Jesus' Jewishness, and the various accusations flung at some scholars, one might get the impression that Jesus' Judaism is a controversial and debated issue; that there are contemporary Chamberlains and Grundmanns in the field actively denying that Jesus is Jewish; or that those who assert Jesus' Judaism are saying something new and controversial. But nothing could be further from the truth. Present-day mainstream scholars of antiquity simply do not deny that Jesus was Jewish. Yes, there are some third-world scholars who repeat some of the now-discredited chestnuts of past scholarly anti-Judaism.[9] And what is true of scholarship may not necessarily be true in general. There are of course obviously anti-Semitic organizations scattered throughout the United States and Canada, some of which claim religious allegiance to Jesus and deny that he was ethnically Jewish. The Church of the Creator is probably the most well-known of these organizations.[10] Less obvious but perhaps more distressing are the numerous people who endorse truly anti-Semitic claims apparently out of ignorance. In Saskatchewan we recently beheld the spectacle of a prominent Cree politician having to resign his position after making comments in public to the effect that Hitler was trying to prevent Germany from being taken over by the Jews, and that the Holocaust was therefore justified (see www.cbc.ca/stories/2002/12/17/ahenakew021217). And historically, anti-Semitism ebbs and flows. Its current political marginality and impotence need not indicate that it is permanently defunct.

But in terms of current, mainstream scholarship in North America and Western Europe, the non-Jewish historical Jesus is a classic straw man, a way of characterizing the views of one's opponents as self-evidently false. This usage in and of itself illustrates precisely how uncontroversial a Jewish Jesus really is: accusing someone of producing a non-Jewish Jesus is generally offered as a *sufficient* critique of their reconstruction—that Jesus might not have been Jewish is self-evidently false, and its falsity is taken for granted in contemporary scholarship. So then why the continued insistence on a point everyone accepts? What is behind the shrill reiteration of Jesus' having been Jewish? What agenda is served by accusing contemporary scholars—with no evidence whatsoever—of an anti-Jewish animus, or of offering sly insinuations to this effect? Why the invocation of the specter of Grundmann—particularly now, when it seems this aspect of our scholarly past has been decisively left behind? The fact is, to reiterate, Jesus' Jewishness is currently *not* under attack, and has not been for several decades. And yet it is under discussion more now than ever. To my mind, this suggests that the issue is somehow overdetermined; it is a screen onto which other, more current, and unresolved matters are being projected. It is a manufactured controversy serving to express other problems, theological and secular, in a covert or implicit manner.

3 A Manufactured Controversy: Why the "Jewish Jesus" is a Red Herring

That the question of the Jewish Jesus is a manufactured controversy may itself be a controversial claim, and so may require some justification. So before moving on to a consideration of the covert issues animating the Jewish Jesus "debate," I wish to focus briefly on some recent historical Jesus scholarship, especially on the work of those deemed to be constructing a "non-Jewish" Jesus, and my reasons for regarding this claim to be an empty one. It is striking that the scholars on the receiving end of this type of criticism are precisely those who have struggled most valiantly to contextualize Jesus—socially, historically, culturally—and so to make him *more* a product of his time. Such a tendency, of course, cuts entirely counter to the tendency to make Jesus *unique*, and so at least in this key respect, is of a piece with the contemporary "Jewish Jesus," and is considerably at odds with the older scholarship, both Christian and anti-Semitic, that emphasizes Jesus' distinction from his context.

A Non-Jewish Jesus?

The scholarship that appears to have been singled out for special criticism as producing a non-Jewish Jesus has tended to be work in which Jesus is associated with Cynicism, or with peasant movements, or in which his Galilean context is given especial emphasis. The chief scholars in question include John Dominic Crossan, Burton L. Mack, Leif Vaage, Richard Horsley, and the Jesus Seminar.[1] One of the more disturbing aspects of these scholars' work is its focus on the Galilee as the immediate context of Jesus' activity. It is worth noting that many of the more vocal critics of these scholars, the proponents of the "Jewish Jesus," tend in their characterizations of Jesus to focus especially on his activities in *Jerusalem*. This allows for a more self-evident applicability of Judaism proper, the temple, purity considerations, and the like. It also allows for an eliding of what differences, religious, cultural, and social, may have existed between Galilee and Judea. E. P. Sanders is the clearest example of this tendency: he regards Jesus' "cleansing" of the temple, an event necessarily located in Jerusalem, to be the key to understanding Jesus' mission and agenda (Sanders 1985); this in spite of the fact that, apparently, most of the activity of the historical Jesus took place in Galilee and the surrounding regions. By contrast, an emphasis on the Galilean context of Jesus' activity was especially cherished by anti-Semites such as Chamberlain and Grundmann: it was Jesus' *Galilean* identity that allowed for inferences about his anti-Jewish message and his non-Jewish ethnicity. In this older, overtly anti-Semitic reconstruction, the Galilean identity of Jesus is used in two main ways: first, through the ideological separation of Galilee from Judea, such that Galileans are imagined to hold religious views that distance them from, especially, Jerusalem; and, second, in the claim that Galilee's chequered history makes it unlikely that it was populated predominantly by ethnic Judeans during Jesus' lifetime. Interestingly, *both* of these claims are flirted with in contemporary historical Jesus work, perhaps most notably in the writings of Jonathan Reed (especially Reed 2000) and Richard Horsley (especially Horsley 1995, 1996), both of whom have engaged in extensive reconstruction of the historical Galilee as a route to inferences about the historical Jesus.[2]

Horsley's view is that Galilee cannot and should not be assimilated to Judea: it has its own history, the course of which was often quite independent of developments to the south, in Judea and Jerusalem. He complains that:

> Since attention in these fields has only recently focused specifically on Galilee, interpretation generally continues within the standard paradigm of "Judaism," "Jewish Palestine," or "Eretz Israel," within which information from or about Galilee was previously understood. Few distinctions of any sort were made, whether geographical or social. Texts and artifacts that happened to come from Galilee were simply assimilated as evidence for an essential "Judaism." In effect, Galilee was rendered almost invisible in historical and archaeological interpretation. (Horsley 1996, 3–4)

If we wish to understand Galilean figures, then, including both Jesus *and* the later rabbis (a juxtaposition and comparison that would have been unthinkable to Chamberlain or Grundmann), we must look to what is distinctive of Galilee itself. Such a perspective tends to distance Galilean religiosity—and thus the presumed religiosity of Jesus himself—from the temple, purity, and Torah which are deemed critical for Judea to the south. And so we learn from Horsley that:

> Age-old indigenous local religious practices and attachments also persisted in Galilee. Unlike Judea, which had been dominated by the Temple and high priesthood in Jerusalem for centuries, Galilee was ruled by a series of imperial regimes and never developed a central sacred place.... Besides such local cultural tradition, Israelite cultural traditions remained strong in Galilee. Once we are aware of the class and regional differences between the Galileans and the governing and scribal circles in Jerusalem ... the

Israelite traditions can no longer be discussed simply in terms of "scripture" or "the Law." The distinction anthropologists often make between the "great tradition" and the "little traditions" may be of some help in formulating the issues. (Horsley 1996, 172–73)

This approach also opens the door to an ethnic differentiation between Galileans and Judeans. Horsley appears to recognize this and shy away from it, claiming that "although some of the inhabitants of Galilean villages may have been of non-Israelite background, most of the Galileans must have been descendants of the northern Israelite tribes" (Horsley 1996, 173; cf. 1995, chs. 1 and 2). But Jonathan Reed has challenged Horsley's views on the Israelite descent of Galileans, arguing strongly (and convincingly) for an ethnic *discontinuity* between the Northern Kingdom's "Israelite" population and any post-Assyrian "indigenous" population (Reed 2000, 28–43). It is notable that either Horsley's or Reed's arguments *could* be used to argue for a non-Jewish ethnic composition of Galilee, depending on how one defines "Jewish." If by "Jewish" one means specifically Judean, then Horsley's views imply a centuries-long divorce between Galileans and Judeans, last living under the same political roof in the time of Solomon. Horsley explicitly rejects claims for large-scale Judean immigration to the Galilee, whether in the Maccabean period or even after the Jewish War (Horsley 1996, 25–28, 40–41, 61–62). Conversely, if by ethnically "Jewish" one means descended from the biblical "Israelites," then Reed is emphatic in denying this status to Galileans.

But it is also notable that such an implication seems very far from— indeed, inimical to—the intentions of both scholars: each is in their own way asserting, precisely, the Jewish ethnicity of the Galilee. For Horsley, this is found (in part) in his ability to trace the Galilean population in the time of Jesus all the way back to biblical Israel. For Reed, it is found in the claim that the Galilee was more or less depopulated by the Assyrians, and was resettled by Judean Jews in the Hasmonean period (Reed 2000, 28–43). Thus while we encounter the same motifs in this work as were exploited by scholars such as Chamberlain and Grundmann, it should be clear that the agenda behind such current work are in no way anti-Jewish or anti-Semitic. Horsley, in explicitly distancing Galilee from Judea, even to the point of raising the question of its ethnic discontinuity with Judea, is conceptualizing those differences in terms of anthropological distinctions between "great" and "little traditions." Neither he nor Reed, most emphatically, are arguing for anything like an "Aryan" Galilee. Reed sums up his conclusions nicely:

Of particular importance to historical Jesus research is the observation that Galilee's essentially Jewish character was shared with Judea. Therefore, speaking of the Galilean Jesus is in no way intended as a contrast to the Jewish Jesus, but simply specifies or qualifies Jesus as a Galilean Jew. The Jewish ethnicity and religion of Galilee has been demonstrated from

> two vantage points—its settlement patterns and the presence of Jewish ethnicity markers there. (Reed 2000, 216–17)

What both Reed and Horsley are doing in their examinations of the local characteristics of Galilee, including an examination of ethnicity, are addressing some of the facts and problems capitalized upon by anti-Semites in the past. The facts and problems persist, and cannot be wished away; the answers, however—and even more importantly, the motivations and general agenda—differ radically. It would be an injustice of the first order to accuse either Horsley or Reed of anti-Semitism. Yet the issues and data they address are precisely those that animated Chamberlain, Grundmann, and their ilk.

Although Burton Mack, on the one hand, and Richard Horsley and Jonathan Reed, on the other, see eye to eye on very little, the emphasis on a distinctive description of Galilee is one matter on which they do agree. Indeed, Mack's conclusions about Galilee appear to agree with Horsley's *only* insofar as they both suggest a distinction between the Galilee and Jerusalem. Horsley's Galilee is peasant-dominated and culturally rather isolated (see, e.g., Horsley 1996, 24); Mack's is cosmopolitan, multi-ethnic, and Hellenized (Mack 1988, 65–66 and n. 9; 1993, 54–58). But both stress not only cultural distinctions between Galilee and Judea, but indeed even cultural *oppositions* between the two (e.g., Mack 2001a, 52–53).

The result in Mack's case is a Jesus who lacks many of the supposed hallmarks of Judean culture; who is not, in short, distinctively or obviously Jewish. Jesus, instead, is a Cynic-like wisdom teacher, who taught in the form of socially critical aphorisms calling individuals to a lifestyle free from social artifice (Mack 1988, 62–64; 1993, 64; 2001a, 48–51). Mack states outright that "The tenor of the teachings [of the historical Jesus] is hardly a good example of strictly Jewish idiom, mentality, and interests untarnished by contact with the Greco-Roman world" (2001a, 55). While it should be stressed—and Mack's critics have failed sufficiently to appreciate this point—that this reconstruction is based on *literary* evidence rather than socio-historical claims about Galilee,[3] Mack concludes that this reconstructed discourse of the historical Jesus does indeed fit with what we know about the Galilee in the first century. In light of Galilee's distinctions from Judea, its placement along trade routes, its cosmopolitanism, and the presence of notable Cynics in the nearby Decapolis, "the correspondence between the Cynics and the discourse of the early stages of the Jesus movement can be acknowledged as plausible and appropriate for Galilee in the early first century" (Mack 2001a, 53).

Three points need to be raised with respect to Mack's reconstruction of the historical Jesus. The first is that the de-Judaization of Jesus that allegedly occurs here, occurs at the behest of *evidence*. Mack, in other words, in his lack of attention to such features of Jewish religiosity as Torah and temple, is not guilty of wish-fulfillment or—as with the likes of Grundmann, even when he was referring to genuinely factual data—of making inferences about Jesus based on generalizations about the Galilee. The evidence in question is actually quite specific: the material that Mack thinks represents the earliest strands of the sayings traditions associated with Jesus, most particularly the aphoristic material in the earliest stage of Q (Q^1) and the material underlying the pre-Markan pronouncement stories (see Mack 2001a, 43–48; cf. 1993, 109–14), simply does not make much of the epic tradition, the Torah, or the temple, and tends to minimize or even criticize purity considerations. In his reconstruction of a Jesus who does not appear concerned with "typically" Jewish considerations, Mack is simply *describing* the contents of the earliest sayings material ascribed to Jesus (see Mack 2001a, 57). He is not starting with a presupposition of who or what Jesus "must" have been, but is basing his conclusions on the evidence that strikes him as most reliable. And even the selection and character of this evidence is not something Mack himself is inventing. That the pronouncement stories in Mark stem from some kind of pre-Markan source is a conclusion going back to the classic form critics, and worked out recently by scholars other than Mack (see Mack 1988, 172–74 and nn. 1–2, citing Tannehill 1981); and the isolation of an early stratum of Q material (Q^1) is primarily the work of John Kloppenborg (see Kloppenborg 1987). Mack himself is not responsible for the generation of the basic evidence that he cites for his image of Jesus. It should follow, then, that those uncomfortable with Mack's reconstruction, for whatever reasons, address the evidence behind it, rather than speculating about Mack's motives or (mis)characterizing his portrait as non-Jewish and therefore, apparently, self-evidently wrong.

The second thing to be noted about Mack's reconstruction of Jesus— and this applies also to Horsley, Reed, and most of those scholars accused of offering a non-Jewish Jesus—is that the accusation ignores what Mack himself actually says about Jesus' Judaism. It is worth stressing that Mack— along with Reed, Horsley, Crossan, Funk, and others—does quite explicitly assert that Jesus was Jewish, that his first followers were Jewish, and that the Galilee in the first century was marked by features of Jewish culture and religiosity: "Jesus was born and raised in Galilee, no doubt from a Jewish family" (Mack 1988, 62). Indeed, Mack stresses the ways in which Jesus' Jewish background led to his approach being *distinct* from that of the Cynics:

> The Cynic analogy repositions the historical Jesus away from a specifically Jewish sectarian milieu and toward the Hellenistic ethos known to have prevailed in Galilee. It reaches its limits, however, when confronted with two additional observations. The first is that the kingdom Jesus represented was theologized. The emphasis upon God as ruler of the kingdom (kingdom *of God*) strikes a note of seriousness a bit unusual for Hellenistic

sensibility. The second is that those who heard him formed groups, all of which understood themselves to be religious movements with claims upon Jewish traditions. A religious piety of some kind must therefore be assumed for Jesus, energized by concerns that can generally be equated with Jewish ethical and theocratic ideals, but lacking interest in specifically Jewish institutions. (Mack 1988, 73–74; emphasis original)

Critics of Mack's version of the "Cynic hypothesis" as non-Jewish are thus forced to ignore what he actually *says* about the Judaism of Jesus, and instead infer that being a Cynic requires that one *not* be Jewish. Such a claim not only requires the assumption that first-century Jews could not think of themselves in terms of the philosophical schools of the Greco-Roman world,[4] but further is predicated on the incorrect assumption that Mack, and other advocates of the "Cynic hypothesis," are claiming that Jesus *was* a Cynic. Aside from occasional sloppy wording (on which see Arnal 2001a, 57), this is simply not so. The point of scholars such as Mack, Vaage, and Seeley in referring to the Cynics is precisely *comparison*, not identity.[5] Thus even if it were impossible for a first-century Jew to *be* a Cynic, this would not necessarily vitiate the point of the comparison. Any critique or rejoinder to the so-called "Cynic hypothesis" must recognize that comparison is the issue here, and frame its response accordingly: is the comparison helpful? Does it tell us anything?

The third and perhaps most important point to be made about Mack's historical scholarship is that, for a change, we do actually have some evidence about his motives. In several of his scholarly writings, Mack makes it clear that the ideology behind "the Christian myth," especially as exemplified in Mark's paradigmatic portrait of Jesus, is one that he finds massively problematic.[6] In particular, he traces many of the more unattractive features of Western history and even contemporary American culture to the narrative logic of the Christian story in its emphasis on the purity and innocence of "us," the righteous (the eponymous "myth of innocence"), and the ways in which all acts of violence are laid at the feet of one's enemies. He hopes to oppose such a constellation of, in his view, dangerous ideas with a more sensible and down-to-earth historical reconstruction, in which humans appear as humans, where mixed motives, flaws, and contingencies are the driving forces of historical change rather than unique geniuses and divine irruptions.

Part of the almost-necessary impact of the Christian myth, part of its essential logic, as far as Mack is concerned, is its anti-Jewish dimension. The innocent Jesus of the myth who breaks into ordinary human history comes with the commission to condemn Judaism, a theme elaborated first in Christian theology, and later in historical scholarship:

> The theory of reformation arises from the history of Christian theology. According to this view, Judaism was badly in need of reform because the

temple-state was based on a priestly system of sacrificial religion that was primitive, embarrassing, and wrong. Or, focusing upon the Pharisees, the religion of Judaism has been characterized as exclusivistic, legalistic, and wrong. Or, reading the Hebrew scriptures as the Old Testament of the Christian Bible, the Jéws had not listened to the prophets, were a disobedient people, and were greatly in need of the messiah lest they fall under the wrath of their righteous God. (Mack 1993, 62)

Speaking, then, of the Christian narrative established by Mark, Mack concludes, quite savagely:

This sorry plot lies at the very foundations of the long, ugly history of Christian attitudes and actions toward Jews and Judaism. The destruction of their city was only a sign. They did not vanish as was their due and thus were there to reap repeatedly the wrath of God in anticipation of the final, apocalyptic resolution. No thinking person can justify this long history, nor doubt that the gospel has justified it in the eyes of Christians. Boring and distasteful, the documents pile up from the time of the early church, through the *adversus Judaeos* literature, to the crusades, reactions to the plagues, Catholic doctrine, Luther's pronouncements, German tracts of the nineteenth and early twentieth centuries, common clichés in New Testament scholarship, and the anomaly of anti-Semitic attitudes that emerge throughout the third world wherever the gospel is read today. The Nazi enactment of the final solution forty years ago may have been tainted by pagan desires. But the rationale was Christian. The holocaust was also a gospel event. (Mack 1988, 375)

Mack's Cynic-like Jesus is at least in some respects an effort to create an *alternative*, a less *dangerous* alternative, to the Markan picture of Jesus.

Regardless of whether Mack is correct or not in his assessment of the impact of "the Christian myth," it should be graphically obvious not only that his agenda is not anti-Jewish, but is, indeed, inspired by a reaction to the anti-Semitism rationalized and generated by Christian theology. Thus even were it true that Mack's Jesus is somehow "non-Jewish," the reason for this—especially the reason that Mack's historical Jesus does not comment on specifically Jewish institutions—is *precisely* his desire to *avoid* a historical Jesus who comes to condemn Judaism and its institutions. In other words, Mack's agenda is not especially different from those who wish to protect and emphasize the Judaism of Jesus: a distaste for the anti-Jewish aspects of Christian history and its story.

Without going into the same detail, it is still worth noting that similar motivations—again, demonstrably—underlie Leif Vaage's Cynic-like Jesus. This agenda is especially marked in his article on the Q woes against the Pharisees (Vaage 1988). Here Vaage argues that the Q woes, taken in subsequent sources and scholarship as a savage indictment of the "legalism" of the Jewish religion, should be understood in Q in terms of a *playful* Cynic-like critique of convention. Note that, as with Mack, the agenda here in characterizing Jesus by comparison to Cynic discourse is not at all to distance Jesus from Judaism somehow, but on the contrary to contextualize his critique as operating *within* Judaism, and especially as lacking the serious and even ponderous weight that has normally been associated with Jesus' message. The woes were not originally a condemnation, they were a set of amused observations on the differences between stated values and life as it is really lived.

One can find similar sentiments expressed, often quite explicitly, in other scholars accused of having produced a non-Jewish Jesus. In the work of the Jesus Seminar, for instance, explicitly compared to Grundmann's scholarship by Birger Pearson, there appears to be both a desire to deny the historicity of episodes and statements supportive of Christian anti-Judaism, and an effort to spell out explicitly the consequences of those episodes and sayings. For instance, in a discussion of the historicity of the Markan presentation of the crowds' repudiation of Jesus before Pilate (Mark 15:1–14), *The Acts of Jesus* states:

> When Pilate asks the crowd what he is to do with "the king of the Judeans," they call out to have him crucified (vv.12-14). There is considerable irony in that scene: the Judeans are now to assume responsibility for the death of someone called their king (v.12). Pilate gives way to the will of the crowd, has Jesus flogged in accordance with Roman practice, and turns Jesus over to his enemies to be crucified. That scene, although the product of Mark's vivid imagination, has wrought untold and untellable tragedy in the history of the relation of Christians to Jews. There is no black deep enough to symbolize adequately the black mark this fiction has etched in Christian history. (Funk and the Jesus Seminar 1998, 153)

Or again, John Dominic Crossan's historical Jesus, who has come under fire for, apparently, not being Jewish enough, is the product of a scholar who has devoted an entire book to the question of the linkage between Christian stories about Jesus and subsequent anti-Semitism, including the Holocaust. Crossan's *Who Killed Jesus?* directly engages, at a historical level, the key Christian claim sitting at the root of nearly 2,000 years of anti-Judaism: the claim that "the Jews" killed Jesus (Crossan 1995). Crossan asserts, predictably enough, that this claim is a fiction, perpetrated by the gospel writers—particularly Mark—in the interests of intra-Jewish polemic. This conclusion is an important one, says Crossan, precisely because of the impact that the claim of deicide, and the Passion narrative that supports it, have had:

> There may well be some stories in the New Testament that one can leave as "maybe historical" and avoid asserting one's best historical judgment or reconstruction about them. But the passion-resurrection stories are different because they have been the seedbed for Christian anti-Judaism. And without that Christian anti-Judaism, lethal and genocidal European

anti-Semitism would have been impossible or at least not widely successful. What was at stake in those passion stories, in the long haul of history, was the Jewish Holocaust. (Crossan 1995, 35)

One could go on at length. It should be evident, however, that not only do scholars such as Vaage, Mack, Funk, and Crossan assert that Jesus was indeed Jewish, but that their characterizations of the historical Jesus are at least in part offered as efforts to *correct* or even compensate for Christian anti-Judaism. Any implications that these scholars are motivated by a covert or overt anti-Judaism, or, worse, anti-Semitism, should be definitely laid to rest by their own words: not simple denials of the charge, but actual demonstrations that quite the opposite is true.

It is therefore not simply surprising, but actually shocking, to encounter characterizations of such scholarship as that recently offered, for example, by John P. Meier:

> Yet, especially among certain authors now or formerly connected with the Jesus Seminar, emphasis on the Jewishness of Jesus is hardly a central concern. Whether one looks at the more serious works of writers like John Dominic Crossan and Burton L. Mack or the sensationalistic popular works of authors like Robert W. Funk, one finds Jesus the Cynic philosopher or Jesus the generic Mediterranean peasant or Jesus the social revolutionary or Jesus the religious iconoclast largely overshadowing if not obliterating the specific 1st-century Palestinian Jew named Jesus. To be sure, words like "Jew" and "Jewish" often adorn titles or subtitles of such works, and politically correct comments are made on the importance of Jesus' Jewishness. But in most of these books, one searches in vain for detailed treatments of various religious movements competing for influence in 1st-century Palestine (e.g., the Pharisees, Sadducees, and Essenes) and of the ways in which Jesus the Jew interacted with or reacted to them as he debated questions of Jewish practice and belief.[7] (Meier 2001, 3–4)

The characterization of Jesus' Judaism in the work of Mack or Crossan as little more than politically correct lipservice is quite unjust; indeed, inexcusable in light of both scholars' explicit repudiation of anti-Judaism in the Christian tradition, as well as the careful and explicit efforts of both Mack and Crossan to analyze and describe the (Jewish) religiosity and culture of Galilee.

This willful disregard of the actual work of these scholars, the dismissal as meaningless ("politically correct" lipservice) of what they actually say, even when the works in question were published years before Meier's comments and so should have been available to him,[8] marks a low point in scholarly discourse on the historical Jesus. It is a nadir approached (though not quite matched), in my opinion, by Sanders's irresponsible recent comments; by Wright's mischaracterizations of Q scholarship; by Pearson's angry essay on the Jesus Seminar.[9] Disrespectful excesses are characteristic of both "sides" in this debate.[10] Again, this is a phenomenon that requires explanation. It is fairly clear on the basis of the slippage from scholarly disagreement to name-calling and misrepresentation that we are dealing with a set of issues around which tempers easily flare. Yet no one is disagreeing that Jesus was Jewish. Why the choler? What is going on?

What is a Jew?

In support of my assertion that the supposed controversy over a Jewish Jesus is no controversy at all, but a manufactured issue, a straw man, I want to draw attention to the fact that a satisfactory definition of just what a Jew is, whether now or, more to the point, in first-century Palestine, has by no means been established. Since *all* parties to the "debate" acknowledge that Jesus was indeed a Jew, formulations such as Meier's or Pearson's, which claim that the Jewish aspects of Jesus are being suppressed or ignored, are simply wrong, perhaps even dishonest. At issue, rather, and obviously, are differing conceptions and constructions of what it *means* that Jesus was a Jew; what *kind* of Jew he was and *how* precisely this affected or impacted on his activity and teaching (so, e.g., Arnal 1997b, 309; Kloppenborg Verbin 2000b, 434, 437; Schüssler Fiorenza 2000, 40). The accusation that some scholars are giving us a non-Jewish Jesus is actually a complaint that he is being cast as the wrong kind of Jew; that his being a Jew is not being presented in the right way. Thus the reason that Meier, for instance, praises Dale Allison, Paula Fredriksen, Bart Ehrman, and N. T. Wright (!), while condemning Crossan, Funk, and Mack (Meier 2001, 3), is categorically *not* because the former assert Jesus' Jewishness while the latter deny it— rather, it is because the former present Jesus' Judaism in a fashion with which Meier agrees, while the latter conceive Jesus' Judaism differently than Meier. Rhetoric aside, then, the controversy, if it is about anything at all, is not about the *fact* that Jesus was a Jew, but about the *nature* of this Jewish identity.

Space here does not permit a thorough investigation of this problem; indeed, the problem may be insoluble. But it is still worth pointing out, however briefly, some of the reasons that the simple assertion that Jesus was a Jew is categorically *not* sufficient to tell us what *kind* of Jew he was; some of the reasons, in other words, that the debate over the kind of Jew Jesus may have been remains a legitimate question. The first and most obvious such reason is the oft-repeated truism that Judaism in the Hellenistic and Roman periods was considerably diverse, socially, culturally, and, yes, even religiously. Just *how* religiously diverse Judaism may have been is a matter of debate, of course, but insisting that, say, comparison between

Jesus and Cynic philosophers makes Jesus non-Jewish goes nowhere toward answering this legitimate question. We may note, with Hengel (1989; cf. Martin 1987, 102–11), that the Judaism of our period, even in Judea but especially in the diaspora, was massively Hellenized, employed the Greek language, proposed comparisons between Judean sects and Greek philosophical schools, and even composed prophecies in the name of the Greek Sibyl. We may note, with Horsley (1996) or Reed (2000), that there are various evidences for Galilean cultural distinction from the practices of Judea; and so we may conclude that there need be nothing anomalous about a Jewish Jesus whose key ideas have much in common with aspects of the Greco-Roman world, or who was not obsessively concerned with the Temple cultus, Torah, or purity issues. Or we may insist, with Freyne (1980), that Galilean religiosity shared the same emphases of Judean piety on temple, Torah, and holy land; and, with Sanders (1992), that there was a form of normative or "common Judaism" in our period that constricted the approved options for Jewish religiosity. These questions are important for defining accurate *generalities* about "Galilean Judaism," and they continue to be debated and debatable. But, again, at issue is not *whether* Jesus, or Galilee in general, were Jewish, but *how*.

Moreover, by insisting that Jesus "must have been" a Jew and that this "must have involved" a focus on, say, the Temple, or on Torah, one runs the risk of making statistical probabilities into certainties, and of turning generalities into caricatures. By foreclosing the question of the distinctions between Galilean and Judean religiosity—by refusing, in other words, to raise the question of the specific ways in which Galilean culture and social life may have impacted on and even vitiated the features normally thought to be necessitated by Judean religiosity—one is essentially claiming that all forms of Judaism must be the same. My point is not that Galilean religiosity *could* not have been more or less identical to that of Judea, nor that claims that it was, based on actual evidence, are making the assumption that all forms of Judaism are or were the same. I am saying, rather, that to refuse to ask the question, to assume without argument or data that Galilean piety *must have been* "Jewish" in the same sense as Judean piety, is operating with the a priori assumption that "Judaism" is a stable and consistent entity. According to such a view, Judaism, instead of being a vibrant cultural tradition with the vicissitudes of human lives as they are really lived, with debates, iconoclasts, surprises; with multiple ways of expressing oneself and one's desires in life; with various and overlapping emphases; with freaks and exceptions—instead of all this, Judaism becomes a lifeless caricature, an unbending mold into which all data must be crammed. Thus the outspoken advocates of the "Jewish Jesus," in insisting on an unrealistic stability to lived Judaism, may, ironically enough, be falling into the same trap as those earlier twentieth-century scholars who presented us with the impoverished caricature of a Jewish religion marked by little else than legalism. A flat set of universal precepts, a two-dimensional foil, comes to replace, in both cases, the variety and vibrancy of actual living human behavior.

Real people—even Jews!—have different views and behave in multiple ways. Serious and sensitive historical scholarship should recognize this, and thus also recognize that generalizations are, precisely, generalizations. Thus even if Freyne is right that generally Galilean Jews were "Torah-true," and even if Sanders is right that there was a form of "common Judaism" in our period, it does not necessarily follow that these generalizations apply to any particular person or group of persons. Some people reject, resist, or deliberately modify key, even definitional, aspects of their culture. Jesus does seem to have spawned a movement, a movement that appears to have departed from "common Judaism" in crucial ways. Without insisting that he be unique, or be understood in "opposition" to "Judaism," we should still note the possibility, even likelihood, that such an influential figure, an apparent catalyst for subsequent change, will be distinctive.[11] Valentinus was a Christian. Siddhartha was a Hindu. Luther was a Roman Catholic. Wovoka was a Paiute. Spinoza was a Jew. And numberless individuals who did not make it into the history books were distinctive in their own ways. In real life, almost everyone fails, in this or that respect, to conform to the statistically predictable generalities of what they *should* be.[12] This does not mean that it is pointless to construct a general picture of Galilean Jewish religiosity. It does mean that such a picture will provide us with a *context* for Jesus' teaching and activity—not with a direct indication of what that teaching and activity *must* have been.

Indeed, as Jonathan Z. Smith has illustrated in a brilliant essay on this very topic, even simply *defining* ancient Judaism is no easy or straightforward matter, and is probably best approached in terms of a polythetic system of classification (Smith 1982b). That is, given the available evidence for ancient Judaism, as well as, especially, the methodological problems inherent in definition and classification, there appears to be no single *one* "differential quality" that marks off Jews as different from their gentile neighbors. Smith formulates the problem by analogy to the definition of walnuts, especially as over against pralines (Smith 1982b, 1–5), and notes that efforts to promote a monothetic definition of the "differential quality" of ancient Judaism "have not been convincing; they have failed to achieve a consensus. They have been poorly formulated and violate the ordinary canons of definition. But this is less disturbing than the fact that the presuppositions of the monothetic enterprise have been deliberately tampered with for apologetic reasons" (1982b, 5). The deliberate tampering in question is the fact that any monothetic definition implies not only that the entity being defined is unique, but also that this uniqueness is a reciprocal phenomenon: if a walnut is unique *vis-à-vis* pralines, then so also pralines are unique *vis-à-vis* walnuts. But definitions of Judaism, especially as over against Christianity, have tended to view the uniqueness of particular religious traditions as non-reciprocal, a point elaborated at greater length and more famously in Smith's *Drudgery Divine* (1990).

In the course of his discussion, Smith examines circumcision as the taxic indicator *par excellence* of ancient Judaism. And he concludes, simply from a brief survey of some of the ancient literary discussions of circumcision, that its significance as a taxic indicator varies from writer to writer (Smith 1982b, 9–14). For some writers, circumcision is both a necessary and sufficient indication that a male is a Jew; interestingly, the strongest ancient proponent of such a view that Smith can find turns out to be Paul (Smith 1982b, 11–12). For other writers, however, circumcision most decidedly does not function as an index of Jewish identity: there seems to have been a *Jewish* "uncircumcision party" reflected in the descriptions and condemnations of texts such as Jubilees 15:33–34 and 1 Maccabees 1:15 (Smith 1982b, 12). And not only did some Jews, apparently, *not* get circumcised, but in addition some non-Jews apparently *did* get circumcised: the practice may have been common, even near-universal, within Judaism, but it was not *unique* to Judaism.[13] Thus Smith notes that the Hadrianic prohibitions against circumcision, for instance, were not directed specifically against Jews or limited to them, but were regarded as a general prohibition against any number of people mutilating their bodies for any number of possible reasons (Smith 1982b, 11). The cross-cultural practice of circumcision may even be taken up into Jewish understandings of the practice, as it seems to have been by Philo: "For Philo, the practice seems to have little to do with either ethnic or religious identity. Circumcision is understood as practiced by intelligent peoples for hygienic reasons" (Smith 1982b, 14). Smith sums up the situation:

> The wide ranges of uses and interpretations of circumcision as a taxic indicator in early Judaism suggests that, even with respect to this most fundamental division, we cannot sustain the impossible construct of a normative Judaism. We must conceive of a variety of early Judaisms, clustered in varying configurations. (Smith 1982b, 14)

He adds, "It is striking that most of the scholars from G. F. Moore to E. P. Sanders, who have pursued the mirage of 'normative Judaism,' ignore the majority of the passages and options considered above" (Smith 1982b, 138 n. 33).

Smith also looks to the evidence of Jewish funerary markers and inscriptions for a sense of ancient Jewish self-definition. Out of the body of 944 grave inscriptions he considers, drawn from Rome, the Galilee, and Egypt, more than three-quarters are in Greek or Latin, and the vast majority of names are Greek or Latin in origin (Smith 1982b, 15). More specifically, Greek is the language used in 70 percent of the inscriptions from Rome, 60 percent from Beth She'arim in Galilee, and 97 percent in Egypt (Smith 1982b, 16). Of this body of 944 inscriptions, only eleven mention God, only eleven mention the Law, only nine use the term "Hebrew," only seven refer to the deceased as a "Jew," only one refers to an "Israelite," and only one refers to "Judaism" (Smith 1982b, 15). Other designations are more common in this corpus: titles designating an office of the synagogue (111); membership in a synagogue (26); reference to the deceased as "pious" (25) or as a rabbi (23, but from the Galilean inscriptions only). Of course, the fact that a trifling 0.84 percent—less than one in one hundred—of these inscriptions identity their honoree with the words "Jew" or "Judaism" may not indicate that this identity was insignificant. Even in the cases of Rome and Alexandria, Jewish identity in a funerary context was probably taken for granted, and more personally distinctive features stressed. But in a way, this is just the point: *within a Jewish context*, being a Jew is not all that salient a detail, and may have little to do with the particular self-conception of any given individual. The iconography on the funerary markers is similarly varied (Smith 1982b, 15–16).[14]

In light of these two key bodies of evidence—the varying treatment of circumcision and the multiplicity of funerary designations—Smith concludes:

> As the anthropologist has begun to abandon a functionalist view of culture as a well-articulated, highly integrated mechanism and has slowly turned to accepting the sort of image … of culture as a "heap of rubbish," a "tangle," a "hotch-potch," only partially organized, so we in religious studies must set about an analogous dismantling of the old theological and imperialistic impulses toward totalization, unification, and integration. The labor at achieving the goal of a polythetic classification of Judaisms, rather than a monothetic definition of early Judaism, is but a preliminary step toward this end. (Smith 1982b, 18)

I have spent so much time on Smith's compact discussion because it is directly relevant to the issue at hand, and is offered by an expert in method and theory in religion, especially in issues of classification. And the question of Jesus as a Jew is precisely a question of classification. Smith's conclusions point to more than simply diversity within ancient Judaism. They also point to the conceptual problems involved in any effort at definition. In particular, his claim that we need to construct and adopt a polythetic classification of plural ancient Judaisms, or, put differently, plural options within Judaism, goes to the heart of the question. If one defines a Jew *as* a Jew because of their adoption of *a large number* of key "Jewish" characteristics, rather than in terms of a single, make or break, index (cf. the approach of Saler 1993, to defining "religion" itself), it follows that being a Jew, identifying oneself as a Jew, and so on, *need* require no single feature of belief or practice. One can thus be a Jew and not be circumcised—indeed, approximately one half of all observant, Orthodox Jews are uncircumcised (I refer, of course, to *women*). One may be Jewish and uninterested in Torah, or the temple, and so on. To be defined as a Jew, one need only adhere to *some* (a greater number than non-Jews) of the defining features of Jewish identity. As a result, defining Jesus as a Jew can tell us nothing specific, at least a priori, about *which* of the classificatory indices make him so.

A matter that Smith does not consider, but that also has bearing on the question is the easy slippage we encounter between "Jew" as an ethnic classification and as a religious classification. Modern examples abound, of course, of ethnic Jews whose ideas and behavior in no way accord with the chief religious features of *any* form of Judaism. Ethnically, Karl Marx was a Jew, as was Sigmund Freud, and for that matter so is Jonathan Z. Smith. One would be hard-pressed to describe the beliefs of any of these figures accurately on the basis of our knowledge that they were of Jewish descent. The situation is as true of antiquity: ethnic background does not foreclose all cultural and ideological options but one. The assertion that Jesus was of Jewish ethnic background, likewise, need not indicate that his life revolved around an analogous religious affiliation. One can hardly doubt, given the tenor of most of the sayings tradition, that Jesus *did* in fact view himself as a Jew in terms of ideology; but this conclusion needs to be established on the basis of the evidence, and cannot be taken for granted on the basis of the fact of Jesus' ethnic identity.

One can go even farther: there is no requirement at all that what was central or distinctive about Jesus had anything to do with what we moderns call "religion." This is an important, if fairly subtle, point. When the step is taken from Jesus the *ethnic* Jew to Jesus the *religious* Jew, what is really being framed is the set of ideological and cultural options that *we today*, as moderns and postmoderns, isolate as "religious." This tendency to assume Jesus was "religious" (without questioning the anthropologically and historically contingent character of that classification) is perhaps most evident in Birger Pearson's complaint that "in robbing Jesus of his Jewishness, the Jesus Seminar has finally robbed him of his *religion*" (Pearson 1996, 43). Similarly, Dale Allison asserts that:

> If Jesus was, for example, either a violent revolutionary or a *secular* sage (neither of which is proposed by any contributor to this book), then the tradition about him, which offers a pacifistic and *religious* sage, is so misleading that we cannot much use it for investigation of the pre-Easter period—and so we cannot know that Jesus was either a violent revolutionary or a secular sage. Here skepticism refutes itself. (Allison in Miller 2001, 26; emphasis added)

The complaint, however, is anachronistic. Several studies have asserted convincingly that in antiquity what we now call "religion" was *embedded* in other aspects of cultural and social life, such as family/kinship and politics (see e.g. Hanson and Oakman 1998, 132–35). The point has also been made more generally that "religion" is a distinctively modern construct, created for and applicable to the western and modern religions of Europe and North America, but inapplicable to either ancient and Medieval culture or to non-Western traditions (Asad 1993; Arnal 2000a, 2001b). Thus when we assert, on the basis of aspects of language that we would call "religious" in the sayings attributed to Jesus or on the basis of the "religious" foci of the movements that followed him, that Jesus' message or action must have been concerned with "religion," we are making a claim that is, anthropologically speaking, simply unsound. Without denying that Jesus may have been and indeed was concerned with certain things we now classify as "religious," we simply cannot use our modern construct of "religion" as a framework for drawing conclusions about what types of issues and practices this "religious" figure, as a religious figure, *must* have cared about, and what issues and practices he must *not* have cared about. The fact that Jesus appears to have talked about "God" need not bring with it a requirement that he also talked about or cared about temple and Torah, or did not, for instance, talk about or care about agriculture or politics or kinship or the role of women. The *necessity* of the former concerns to a religious viewpoint, and the *exclusion* of the latter from a religious viewpoint, are inferences that can be made for no historical epoch except our own. The shortcut from a Jewish Jesus to a "religious" Jesus relies on a distinctively modern and in fact anachronistic classification of religious discourse. Indeed, ironically enough, it relies on a definition of religion that is Protestant in its inception and focuses on individual and personal commitments, inner feelings, and ideational content at the expense of ordinary behaviors and customary actions. Geza Vermès, for example, emphasizes faith, *imitatio dei*, and individualism as key aspects of the "religion" of Jesus (Vermès 1993, 12, 47–49, 184–207). The application of a fundamentally Protestant conception of "religion" to ancient Judaism should be cause for some concern.

I am not claiming, of course, that the descriptions of first-century Judaism by "Jewish-Jesus" advocates are actually too Protestant in their content (although this may be true, in some cases). My claim is that the *types* of actions, beliefs, and behaviors that tend to get classified as part of a "religious" system, as opposed to culture at large, are dictated by a definition that assumes Protestant religiosity as normative (see also Asad 1993). Thus, for instance, since we moderns see devotion, understood as personal commitment, to a deity as an aspect of religion, but do not, for instance, normally see economic behavior as such, we tend to assume that Jesus, as a Jew, could not have worshiped Pan or Herakles, even though cult centers for such deities were *physically closer* to his field of activity than was the cult center of Yahweh. On the other hand, that Jesus probably handled

Tyrian *money* routinely—which normally bore representations of Melqart/ Herakles—does not appear to be a matter of controversy at all.

Linked to this reification of both Judaism as a religious tradition and religion as a distinctive type of cultural behavior see'ms to be a strong reluctance either to engage in any cross-cultural comparisons, or to contextualize Jesus in any ways *other* than in terms of a reified religious context. That is, the scholars who insist that Jesus' Judaism is a starting point from which to make inferences rather than an incomplete claim requiring elaboration, who criticize Crossan or Mack or Vaage for giving us a "non-Jewish" Jesus, appear to be asserting more than simply that Jesus' Judaism is a significant aspect relevant for understanding him. They seem to be claiming, rather, that it is the *only* important aspect relevant for understanding him. The most extreme form of this desire to narrow the focus on Jesus only to his "religion" is most obvious in the accusations that the Jesus of Crossan is too "generic," and could be "any" Mediterranean figure. Freyne, for instance, criticizes Crossan for the "atopicality" of his Jesus (Freyne 1997, 67–68). Even were these claims true, it is hardly a significant criticism unless one assumes that broad cultural contextualization is a bad idea. I see no reason to assume this. Jews, too, were part of the Mediterranean world described by Crossan, and so this description may help us to flesh out "Jesus the Jew" in an anthropologically responsible way.

So also with cross-cultural comparisons, which are, precisely, *cross-cultural*. In endeavoring to compare Jesus the (Jewish) peasant to peasant and other colonial cultures worldwide, the agenda is obviously not to deny that Jesus was Jewish and to claim that he was, say, Indonesian. The point, rather, is that the anthropology of Indonesian peasants may in fact shed light on peasant culture in general, and thus give us valuable new information for understanding the particular peasant culture of the Galilee. This comparative agenda is likewise behind the so-called "Cynic hypothesis," and yet for reasons that I utterly fail to understand, the simple point that comparison neither requires nor even suggests identity appears to have been missed by most (in fact, nearly all) critics of a Cynic-like Jesus. The only possible objection to such a comparative procedure would be to claim that first-century Jews were so utterly *sui generis* that their culture was completely unique and had no points of similarity to any other cultures, past or present.[15] Such a view is indefensible, of course, and would in any case require that we—who are not ourselves first-century Jews—abandon any effort to understand this bizarre and extra-human culture.

It is clear that the assertion that Crossan's (and Mack's, for that matter) contextualization of Jesus in terms of a broad Mediterranean anthropology is too widely focused is a rather ironic claim, coming from "Jewish-Jesus" advocates. I say this because often such scholars themselves tend to contextualize Jesus within a broad "Judaism" that assumes Judean practices as normative and does not pay very much attention to regional differences. Both Fredriksen and Sanders, for instance, tend to conceptualize the "Judaism" of Jesus in terms of the centrality of sacrifice and the temple cultus (Fredriksen 1999, 47–50, 52; Sanders 1992, 45–118; 2002, 38–39). But for *Jews*, at least, sacrifice and temple worship were only available in one (authorized) location, Jerusalem. Does this mean that Galilean Jews *only* expressed their religiosity or felt themselves to be devout and pious on those rare occasions when they visited the Temple? Vermès, at least, recognizes this problem: "As regards Temple worship, it is important to emphasize that although considered the holiest of all religious pursuits by the priestly authorities, such as Simeon the Righteous, and their partisans, it was of the least tangible significance for lay Jews residing away from Jerusalem" (Vermès 1993, 185).

Ironically enough, the focus of these descriptions is too broad; what is needed is an additional focus on distinctively Galilean ramifications of Judean religious practices. Such a focus is provided by scholars such as Crossan, who, however, is accused of being too broad (e.g. by Freyne 1997)! What has happened here, I think, is that scholars such as Sanders or Meier or Fredriksen have assumed that a "religious tradition" is a more or less fixed conceptual frame, and is valid in and of itself as a framework for analysis. Focusing on the broader *culture* of which that tradition is a part, or focusing on trajectories and fissures *within* that tradition, may be viewed, from such a perspective, as either too generalizing or as fracturing a unified entity. Crossan, Mack, Horsley, and others know better, steeped as they are in the theory of cross-cultural comparison, much of it developed in anthropological circles: religion is an aspect of culture, often arbitrarily distinguished, which requires tools and lenses to understand appropriately, and which may, and indeed must, be viewed from multiple perspectives.

Trivializing Anti-Semitism

I have tried here to indicate some of the reasons why I think the criticisms launched at scholars such as Crossan, Mack, Funk, Vaage, and others of producing a "non-Jewish" Jesus are invalid. By this I do not simply mean that such scholars in fact *intend to* and *do* offer us a Jewish Jesus, and that claims to the contrary are blatantly misrepresenting their work, although this is true as well. But what strikes me as of even greater import is that the charges of a "non-Jewish" Jesus appear to be based on a definition of Judaism that is insupportable. It is contradicted by the actual evidence, it is theoretically misguided, and it is anachronistic.

More than this, when charges such as these are leveled against scholars such as Mack and Crossan, or the Jesus Seminar, it trivializes real anti-Semitism, and, as a corollary, racism in general. These kinds of accusations are often offered in lieu of real engagement with the issues and evidence raised by such scholars. One can ignore, for instance, the literary evidence Mack cites in support of his Cynic-like Jesus simply by dismissing the final product as "non-Jewish" and therefore intrinsically implausible. "The Jewishness of Jesus is a phony issue. The accusation that the Jesus Seminar strips Jesus of his Judaism is a powerful attention-getter. But it is an accusation without specific content" (Miller 1999, 75). A nice rhetorical move, to be sure, but one that, as the boy who cried wolf discovered, may have unforeseen consequences. If the charge of "anti-Semite" can be leveled, by implication, at the likes of Robert Funk and the Jesus Seminar, an erudite, well-meaning, and rather innocuous group, then how seriously can the charge be taken when applied to real anti-Semites such as Jean-Marie Le Pen or Ernst Zundel? It seems to me that this charge is an extremely serious one, and should be reserved for serious and dangerous situations. To do otherwise is to degrade the currency. To invoke the charge as a rhetorical *tour de force* in debate about the historical Jesus is to trivialize it beyond belief.[16]

4 The Jewish Jesus and Contemporary Identity

In spite of my extended discussion so far, the issue around which this text centers is neither the anti-Semitic scholarship of the past, nor justifications for or criticisms of current historical Jesus scholarship. Rather, the focus here is on the *agenda* that lurks beneath the supposed "Jewish Jesus" controversy, the *subtexts* that seem to be animating current scholarship, including the acrimony that sometimes characterizes that scholarship. If indeed, as I have claimed, there *is* no current controversy over whether Jesus was Jewish, why are so many scholars talking about it, and in such heated tones? One could argue, of course, that the differences in opinion are caused by one group of scholars being right and the other being wrong in their differing assessment of both Jesus' Judaism and of the work of their scholarly colleagues. At this point it should be clear which group I would identify as "right" and which as "wrong," were I to take this approach. The fact is, I actually have many problems with the substance of Mack's, Crossan's, and the Jesus Seminar's reconstruction of the historical Jesus, but I do think that especially the first two are employing the right kinds of approaches, specific results notwithstanding.

But this is obviously too prejudicial an approach; and it explains nothing, especially why this debate is so *heated* and, at times, downright uncivil. An approach to the subjects that animate this scholarship—treating "Judaism" as something of a cipher for other, unstated, issues of concern; to use psychoanalytic language, a displacement, a manifest content both concealing and expressing a latent content—strikes me as potentially fruitful. As I have already noted, at times scholarship criticizing this or that version of the historical Jesus reflects genuine and legitimate questions about the character of first-century Judaism behind a dichotomous framing of a non-Jewish versus Jewish Jesus. Perhaps looking to *other* issues being reflected in the non-issue of Jesus' Judaism will help clarify some of the *real* differences between historical Jesus scholars, and indeed even lead the way to a more genuinely academic and, one would hope, fruitful, debate.

Two caveats need to be noted from the start, however. The first is that an endeavor such as this is necessarily speculative: I do not have direct access to the inner motives behind scholarly assertions about the past; indeed, I have above characterized some forms of such speculation as irresponsible. I must stress, then, that in what follows I am not especially concerned with the personal and individual motives of the scholars advancing the views I discuss. Rather, my concern is with the ideological resonance of those views; their implications; their correlation with important perspectival issues; their effect on the way we view certain broad issues, and vice versa: the effect on our scholarly conclusions of the way we view certain issues. In general, I do not want to get deeply involved in questions of cause and effect. For example, if scholarship focusing on Jesus as a religious devotee of (a normative) Judaism shares certain key assumptions with, say, contemporary efforts to entrench the boundaries of religious traditions, this *need* not mean: (a) that the scholar in question intended this correspondence; (b) that the contemporary trend caused the historical conclusion; or (c) that the historical conclusion must influence the contemporary trend. Any one, or for that matter all, of these conclusions *may* be true, but the simple correspondence between scholarly claims and present issues does not *require* any of them. My intent in what follows is to point to the correspondences I see, and unless there is direct evidence that allows for a more trustworthy conclusion about motives, I will simply focus on the correspondences and subtexts I see. One need not pin things down further. The important thing about all of these scholars is not what they personally believe, but the kind of *cultural work* their scholarship accomplishes, intended or not.

The second caveat is this: my tendency is to see scholars such as Mack, Crossan, the Cynic-like Jesus advocates, and the Jesus Seminar as being much closer to the truth in their approach to the historical Jesus than those scholars who emphasize Jesus' (religious) Judaism at, it seems to me, the expense of an appropriately critical approach to the gospels or a proper theoretical approach to ancient culture. Thus I am preliminarily or viscerally inclined, when discussing subtexts, to attribute them all to this latter group of scholars, and blithely assume that the Macks and Crossans are simply right, with no further explanation needed. But, as I noted above, this is an inappropriate approach. Even if, say, Burton Mack is wholly correct in his approach to Jesus (an assertion that is unlikely to carry much weight with my interlocutors), that hardly means he has no agenda, no subtexts, no key assumptions behind his work. So in what follows, I will *attempt* to be as even-handed as possible in describing both "sides" of the "debate" as being concerned with, or as engaging, these subtexts. If I insist, for instance, that one set of scholars is using a particular image of Judaism to argue for clearly defined cultural boundaries in our world, it should follow, at least in many cases, that scholars with an opposing image of first-century Judaism may be arguing, covertly, for a loose definition of contemporary cultural boundaries. In what follows, I will *try* to maintain this even-handed approach to the subtexts I see at issue in this discussion. I should note, however, that I myself am far from neutral, either in terms of the stated scholarly conclusions being debated here, or in terms of the subtexts that may serve as their latent content.

Scholarly Identities

The first covert or implicit agenda that may be lurking behind the Jewish Jesus non-debate could be the effort to save our *scholarly* souls from the erstwhile dominance of European and particularly German New Testament scholarship. Up until the 1970s or 1980s the conclusions, the main techniques, and the key figures of productive New Testament scholarship originated, one way or another, in Germany. The whole "second/new quest" was the product of Bultmannian, post-Bultmannian, or Bultmann-trained scholars. Ernst Käsemann, who is credited with opening the "new quest," was a Bultmann student, and originally delivered his address on the historical Jesus to the "Old Marburgers." James M. Robinson's *New Quest of the Historical Jesus* opens with a discussion of Bultmann and of "post-Bultmannian" tendencies in the German scholarship of the 1950s (1959, 9–25). While Robinson was born in the United States, and his Ph.D. was from Princeton, his D. Theol. was from Basel. Norman Perrin, another important American figure in the second quest, was not a student of Bultmann's, but seems to be an exception that proves the rule: he was a student of Jeremias. Likewise, the key techniques and conclusions of Bultmannian scholarship on the historical Jesus—particularly: (a) its focus on the sayings of Jesus as the key to understanding him (see Perrin 1967); (b) the criterion of (double) dissimilarity as the technique for identifying authentic sayings material (Perrin 1967, 39–43); and (c) its considerable skepticism about the historicity of any of the gospel material, especially narrative but also sayings materials[1]—were the most notable hallmarks of most serious historical Jesus studies undertaken especially in the 1950s and 1960s, whether by American or European scholars.

Starting in the 1970s and 1980s, this all changed, and with a vengeance. Anglophone (especially North American, Irish, and British) scholarship came of age, began to find its own legs, and reflected a new confidence. One of the indications of that new confidence was an Oedipal breaking away from the dominance of the field's German forefathers. The trend is even more marked today. This breaking away from German New Testament scholarship, however, did not and does not simply take the form of citing Rudolf Bultmann and his students a little less frequently. It also takes the form of evolving a new set of approaches to the New Testament documents, building on past scholarship, but decisively rejecting some of its more distinctive features. This new, particularly North American, approach to ancient Christianity is signaled decisively in the first few pages of E. P. Sanders's *Jesus and Judaism*,[2] in his rejection of the sayings tradition as the appropriate port of entry to the historical Jesus (Sanders 1985, 4), a concomitant turning to gospel narrative, and of course the assumption that the gospel narratives can be trusted to at least some degree. Indeed, Sanders's list of "indisputable facts" about the historical Jesus in *Jesus and Judaism* (Sanders 1985, 10–11) is little more than an outline of the narrative sequence of the synoptic gospels. The approach of scholars such as Sanders has avoided the most distinctive hallmarks of the so-called "new (second) quest," and it is presumably for this reason that historical Jesus scholarship from the 1980s onwards has been referred to as constituting a *third* quest (see Neill and Wright 1988). The key features of this third quest appear to be, precisely, a *general* acceptance of the accuracy of the gospel narratives, and the application of something like a criterion of *plausibility*—that is: is such an event, saying, or situation likely in terms of what we know about first-century Judaism, and, if so, what would it have meant in that context? Plausibility thus serves as both a mechanism for determining historical authenticity and as a hermeneutical device. No serious scholars of ancient Christianity accept the historicity of *everything* in the canonical gospels. But it appears that "third quest" scholars most often assume that, barring clear evidence to the contrary, the material in the gospels does reflect actual historical events. In other words, the burden of proof rests with those *denying* the authenticity of the material; exactly the opposite approach is normally taken by scholars operating within the "second quest" paradigm, where the burden of proof is on those who *assert* authenticity.

What has developed here is not simply a new technique, but one that works emphatically at odds with the older mode of historical Jesus reconstructions. Not only is the general degree of historical skepticism different in each approach, nor again is it only the case that each focuses on a different body of evidence (sayings versus narrative), but, most strikingly, the key criteria for isolating and interpreting "authentic" material are diametrically opposed, one seeking precisely a *lack of fit* between traditions and their context, the other seeking precisely a *good fit* between tradition and context. And of course the resultant picture of Jesus will be radically different: consistent and exclusive application of the criterion of dissimilarity will lead to a Jesus who is strikingly odd. Thus Robinson complains, "What concerns me most about the Jesus Seminar is that it tends to make Jesus into a queer duck rather than a serious person worthy of a hearing" (Robinson 1996, 46). Conversely, consistent and exclusive application of plausibility, to the exclusion of any criterion of distinctiveness, will present us with a Jesus indistinguishable from any of his contemporaries. The problems with *this* extreme are nicely summarized by Robert Miller:

> If Jesus' speech was not distinctive in his own Jewish context, then why did people bother to remember it and pass it on? If it is not distinctive vis-à-vis later Christian speech, then, by definition, we cannot distinguish

the voice of Jesus from the voice of the church, and therefore the quest for the historical Jesus is futile. So if you accept the viability of historical Jesus research, you cannot avoid the criterion of distinctiveness. (Miller 1999, 75)

As already noted, the more prominent scholars of the so-called "second quest" were either German or trained by Germans. With the "third quest," by contrast, we are dealing not simply with anglophone (either North American, British, or Irish) scholars, but specifically with scholars actually trained in the UK or North America, and by other British or North American scholars. This contrast is made explicitly by Vermès:

> Owing to the colossal influence of Bultmann on German, and subsequently through his former students on North American, New Testament learning, the clock of real historical research stopped for almost half a century, but in the 1950s a modest "new quest" was launched in Germany and in 1956 a Bultmann pupil, Günther Bornkamm, dared to publish a book entitled, *Jesus of Nazareth*…. Several books written in the last twenty years, three of them in Oxford, assert that we can [know something significant about Jesus]. Unlike Bultmann and his followers, the authors of this latest historical quest, while investigating the subject from within the (Synoptic) Gospels, pay not mere lip service to the essential contribution of post-biblical Jewish literature to a genuine perception of Jesus, but in their various ways make substantial use of it. (Vermès 1993, 2–3)

Moreover, scholars singled out as producing a "non-Jewish" Jesus are often also the same scholars accused of falling back on, or regressing to, "second quest" techniques in their reconstruction of Jesus. Pearson, for instance, describes the use of the criterion of distinctiveness (dissimilarity) as a "holdover from the old 'New Quest'" (Pearson 1996, 16). The Jesus Seminar, of course, is the prime example here, with its emphasis on the criterion of dissimilarity, its initial (but not exclusive) focus on the sayings tradition, and its general skepticism about the historical reliability of the gospel material.[3]

I cannot help but speculate, then, that at least some of the anxiety generated over the "Jewish Jesus" derives its energy from a desire to produce a distinctive and, especially, an independent anglophone New Testament scholarship. As we have seen, the classic second-quest scholars tended to produce not simply non-Jewish Jesuses, but practically anti-Jewish ones (and this in the shadow of the Shoah and the Second World War), as can be seen in the work of, for example, Bultmann, Käsemann, Perrin and Duling, and Jeremias, as discussed above. I would deny, of course, that second-quest techniques or key assumptions must *necessarily* lead to a non-Jewish Jesus, or that they were intended to. But it is notable that the two did go hand in hand, at least in the past. The assertion of a thoroughly Jewish Jesus, one who is not measured in terms of his distance from Judaism, but rather his proximity to it, has the effect of making our more recent and homegrown scholarship very distinctive, most especially from our German predecessors. This is all the more so when the very techniques they used are repudiated or even, in some instances, actually inverted.

What we see, then, in the work of scholars such as Vermès, Sanders, and Fredriksen, among others—and this is over against the work of Mack, Crossan, and the Jesus Seminar—is a sharp substantive *and* methodological distinction from their intellectual forebears in the field. Since a general methodological confidence in the synoptic narratives is combined in this scholarship with an insistence on the coherence between Jesus and a generalized "Palestinian Judaism"—a combination that is by no means logically required, since the synoptic accounts can be read as *distinguishing* Jesus sharply from his contemporaries—the distinction from the German schools of New Testament scholarship could not be clearer (so also Schüssler Fiorenza 2000, 40, who likewise insists on the distinctively North American character of the "third quest"). As Mack notes, North American scholarship in particular has gone through three key stages in its approach to Christian biblical texts: a general ignorance of European scholarship; a wholesale embrace of that scholarship; and, finally, a modification of that scholarly edifice to address American concerns (Mack 2001b, 28–30). Mack states that:

> In Europe, New Testament study had been a rigorous academic discipline for over 150 years. During the fifties, European and American scholars trained in Europe were invited to leading positions in graduate schools in the States, bringing with them the lore, rules, and rudiments of European intellectual traditions. It required, however, another fifteen or twenty years before scholars trained and working in America found a way to focus their newly learned critical skills upon questions appropriate to the American scene. (Mack 2001b, 29–30)

It does not really matter for our purposes what these particular "appropriate" questions might have been. What is important here is that Mack is pointing to a kind of coming of age for especially American scholarship on Christian origins. It is difficult not to see in the Jewish Jesus a kind of breakaway, and even repudiation, of the work of earlier German scholarship, paving the way to a new identity and a new confidence for Anglo-American New Testament scholarship, but bringing with it a concomitant danger of throwing out the baby with the bathwater.

It is worth noting, too, that this new identity is also associated with a secularization of the field. The best New Testament scholarship of the first half of the twentieth century was not only undertaken by Germans, but, more specifically, by German Lutherans, who believed their work to have theological relevance and, indeed, to be a theological inquest in itself. More recent anglophone scholarship has been undertaken from a variety of religious perspectives—Christian, Jewish, and wholly secular—and has tended to conceptualize itself as historical rather than theological work:

> Unlike the "new quest," the more recent discussion is not simply an "in-house" Christian debate over the role of historical-Jesus knowledge in Christian faith and theology, but is now a more diverse enterprise involving scholars of various orientations and with broader or more diverse hermeneutical agenda. (Hurtado 1997, 274)

The Jewish Jesus must surely be associated with this less theological, or at least less overt and consistent theological, orientation in recent research. In order to stress the distance between the (illegitimate) theological drive behind earlier work and the (legitimate) historical drive behind more recent work, there may be a tendency to *avoid* presenting Jesus in terms that are continuous with Christianity. In other words, Jesus the Jew is most decidedly not Jesus the Christian, and so demonstrates a non-theological commitment on the part of scholars who present him thus. Many of us are, after all, looking for legitimacy for our field now in the non-confessional setting of the secular university: how better to demonstrate that than to visibly *undo* the theologically-driven "Christianization" of Jesus?

I should be careful to stress that these particular agenda—both the development of a new, progressive, and genuinely North American (or anglophone) brand of New Testament scholarship; a break from and advance from our German predecessors; and the secularization of our field—are agenda with which I am *wholly* in sympathy. Indeed, I tend to agree with those scholars who have jettisoned criteria such as dissimilarity or distinctiveness as unworkable,[4] and who have noted that the sayings tradition does not give us any controllable or solid access to the original teachings of the historical Jesus (so, famously, Sanders 1985, 16–17). I agree with this conclusion, but not with the implications scholars such as Sanders draw from it; as far as I am concerned, the narrative tradition is a much, much *worse* source for the historical Jesus. My problem with the sayings tradition is that I simply cannot figure out how, once one peels away literary and other accretions to the material and arrives at the earliest form, one can take the final step and assign the saying to Jesus. In short, while I do think we can often reconstruct the "earliest" form of much of the sayings material, I am not nearly so confident that there is any reason at all to connect these reconstructed sayings with the historical Jesus.

For that matter, I am in agreement with the wholesale rejection of an earlier scholarship's reconstruction of a Jesus so distinctive—necessarily distinctive, because he is the son of God—that he cannot appear similar to his contemporaries in any significant or meaningful respect, including in his Judaism (however that be conceived). I think that the foreseeable future of Christian origins will in fact be found in anglophone universities and no longer in German seminaries and theological faculties. We are, quite successfully, assimilating some of the lessons of the past, and also building upon its successes. No longer content either to repeat the historical conclusions of Bultmann, nor to subordinate our historical work to edifying exegesis, we are carving out new territory. The Jewish Jesus is part of that territory, though, I would insist, not all of it. This figure, as it appears in the work of Fredriksen or of Sanders, is a figure Bultmann and his students could and would never have come up with. It is a new hypothesis, home-grown on American (and Canadian, Irish, and UK) soil; not a footnote or a genuflect to the past of our field. In this, at least, the work of Vermès, Fredriksen, and Sanders deserves a place alongside that of, for instance, Burton Mack. All of these scholars are presenting us with new, forward-thinking hypotheses; are rejecting the outmoded use of an inapplicable criterion of distinctiveness; and appear to be operating from a secular perspective. I would not want us to go back.

But at the same time, a certain amount of care is required that, in slaying our fathers,[5] we do not rob ourselves of their inheritances, especially when those inheritances may be quite valuable. As it happens, the German scholarship that we are so wont to reject as we invent our own went through a series of stages during which a great deal was learned. The skepticism of a Bultmann was not pulled out of thin air: it was based on the results of nearly a century of futile historical Jesus reconstructions as well as the conclusions of source- and form-criticism. If all we are doing is reinventing the wheel on this side of the Atlantic (or the Channel), what we will end up with, after fifty or a hundred years, is, precisely, another wheel. Why bother? It seems to me that we can still produce our own distinctive—and secular—mode of scholarship even while building on some of the insights of the scholars who preceded us, as well as while learning from their mistakes. Attempting to behave either as though such scholarship never existed, or simply inverting all of its conclusions and methods, will not serve us well. Our scholarly identities will best be served by hard work and honesty; not by a facile repudiation of all the work of the past.

And—to continue my invocation of Freudian metaphors—there is always the danger of a return of the repressed. Somehow, things become strangely inverted, and our desire to escape the theological agenda of Protestant exegetes such as Bultmann may actually be providing fodder to scholars whose agenda is even more aggressively theological. The rejection, in particular, of Bultmannian skepticism—even though that skepticism *was* in part theologically determined—is no great advance for secular and historical approaches to Christian origins. No, by contrast, and ironically, scholars such as Sanders, Fredriksen, and Vermès have, in their openness to synoptic historicity, provided solace to theologically-driven scholars such as N. T. Wright, Richard Hays, and Ben Witherington. Indeed, often the former scholars are associated with the latter and thus lend them legitimacy (see, e.g., Meier 2001, 3). Thus in an understandable desire to distance ourselves from the theological agenda of Bultmannianism, we run the risk of opening the doors wide to the more conservative, less creative, and ultimately historically dishonest approaches of theologues whose only agenda is to use historical rhetoric to demonstrate the "truth" of Christianity. This is a real threat, a real danger. If our field is ever going to be drawn down to perdition, this will be the route it takes: a capitulation to the anti-scholarly ethos of the True Believers, a disdain for any sort of historical inquiry that may call into question the "real" Jesus of faith and dogma (e.g., Johnson 1996; for an excellent critique, see Miller 1999, 79–108).

Political Identities

A much easier undercurrent to track is the political agenda behind the "controversy" over a Jewish Jesus. Moreover, it is an easier undercurrent to verify. The fact is, a great many works which emphasize the "Jewish Jesus," and especially which criticize scholars such as Crossan or Mack for producing an allegedly "non-Jewish" Jesus make *explicit* reference to anti-Semitism, and to the great anti-Semitic event of the twentieth century, the Shoah. Seán Freyne, for instance, is very straightforward and open about this connection (Freyne 1997, 91). So are others. The subtitle, for instance, of Fredriksen and Reinhartz's *Jesus, Judaism, and Christian Anti-Judaism* (2002) is, significantly, "Reading the New Testament after the Holocaust" (cf. also Vermès 1993, 213–15). What is especially interesting is that this connection will be made even when their authors explicitly disavow any anti-Semitic motivation in those they criticize. Thus Pearson's critique of the Jesus Seminar invokes the genuinely anti-Semitic scholarship of the Nazi period and surmises that the Seminar's "non-Jewish" Jesus "might arouse some disquiet in the minds of people who know the history of the 30's and 40's of our century" (Pearson 1996, 42). But immediately he goes on to say that "the Jesus of the Jesus Seminar is much too banal to cause us to think that the ideology producing him is like that which produced the 'Aryan Jesus' of the 1930's" (Pearson 1996, 42). Likewise Sanders, who does assert that "genuine anti-Judaism ... has been a feature of many scholarly descriptions of Jesus" (Sanders 2002, 54), nonetheless believes that the unspecified scholars who promote this anti-Judaism do not do so out of any specific anti-Semitic animus but from a general distaste for ancient religiosity (Sanders 2002, 34–35). That such a concern—whether with Nazi ideology or with generalized anti-Semitism and anti-Judaism—is invoked, only immediately to deny its applicability, is a strong indication that it rests heavily in the minds of the scholars who mention it. As with our scholarly identities, so also we are attempting to distance our political identities from Germany as well—this time, however, from the Germany of Adolf Hitler, not of Rudolf Bultmann.

What is at issue here, at a political level, is a scholarly, narrative, and symbolic repudiation of anti-Semitism among those researchers who insist on a Jesus whose Judaism is identifiable *as* Judaism even today. Crossan's Jesus is a Jew; as is Mack's, and Vaage's, and the Jesus Seminar's. But Jesus the Jew in *these* avatars is not easily identifiable with or conformable to the Jews of today, the Jews of modern Israel, or especially the Jews of Eastern Europe, the primary victims of Hitler's genocide. Conversely, those who wish to portray an ancient Judaism that is obvious and identifiable present Jesus as a Jew who is concerned with the Temple and with the city of Jerusalem, both potent symbols of an "exiled" Jewry even after the destruction of 70 CE. We are given a Jesus focused on Torah; a Jesus proximate to but segregated from his Gentile neighbors. Galilee was ringed with Gentile cities, but the "Jewish Jesus" advocates insist that he understood his mission as devoted exclusively to Jews, implying an interesting parallel to the modern circumstances of European Jews: surrounded by Gentiles, but segregated. We find in this scholarship a Jesus who was circumcised; who wore distinctively Jewish clothing and religious paraphernalia; and who had a recognizably Jewish name (i.e., Yehoshua or Yeshua), this latter in spite of the fact that all of our early sources call him *Jesus* (but see Matthew 1:21). Bruce Chilton (1984) characterizes Jesus as, precisely, a Rabbi. The gospels use this term from time to time, but as a respectful address (the term occurs fifteen times in the entire New Testament, but only in Mark, Matthew, and, pre-eminently, John). Chilton, using the term the way he does, implies a clerical role, one associated, of course, with modern Judaism. It is conceivable, though perhaps stretching the point, to see in Vermès's "charismatic" Jesus (1973) an evocation of modern Hasidism.

A Jesus described in these terms shows enough similarity and continuity to the type of the nineteenth- to twentieth-century European Jew as to stand in for this latter historical figure. Nowhere is this more clear than the jacket of Paula Fredriksen's *Jesus of Nazareth* (1999), which features a painting by Marc Chagall of a crucified Jesus surrounded by figures in Eastern European garb ("White Crucifixion," 1938). Chagall can be forgiven his artistic license: this is a painter, after all, who presents us with naked figures riding giant roosters, faces in the sky, and floating buildings. But Chagall's amazing vision is not history. The cover of a book is not necessarily an indication of the scholarship inside the book, and in some instances cover art is even beyond the author's control. But in this case, whether the cover art was chosen by Fredriksen or not, I believe it tells us something about the conceptualization of both Jesus and of Judaism that one finds in this book, and even hints at some of the reasons for these conceptualizations. The characters in "White Crucifixion" are clearly not enjoying themselves: at least not those fleeing and having their houses burnt down.

The Eastern European Jew is the very image of anti-Semitic stereotype; he or she is "the eternal Jew" of Hitlerian propaganda. The figure who resists assimilation, is segregated, obeys distinctive ancestral law, speaks in an incomprehensible and "foreign" language written in an incomprehensible and "mystical" alphabet, eats differently, dresses differently—such a figure can stand in easily as a target for any xenophobia whatsoever. Who is the outsider lurking within? Who is the yeast that leavens the whole loaf? Who is the subversive, the communist, the usurer? Why, of course, the Jew: who else could it be? And how do we know? Because "the Jews" self-present as outsiders in their whole way of life. Thus a particularly segregated Jewish subculture, that of central and eastern European Ashkenazi Jews, comes to symbolize Judaism in general, and, at the same time, to be the quintessential target for intolerance, racism, and religious and socio-cultural prejudice emanating from European (and subsequently, too, North American) Gentiles.

The fact that the very distinguishability of Eastern European Jewry is what it seems most to share with the Jewish Jesus of recent scholarship—language, law, clothing, distinctive practice, lack of assimilation, segregation—suggests to me that Jesus himself is being made to conform to a stereotype of Judaism that was anti-Semitic in its inception. But this, I suspect, is no irony: it is precisely the point. The very center of (anti-Jewish and, at times, anti-Semitic) European culture has been the figure of Jesus. The historically dominant religion(s) of Europe have revolved around this Jesus; its art has portrayed him ceaselessly; its architecture been offered to his greater glory; its literature has aimed at exegeting his importance or explaining him to the masses. How better, then, to repudiate the anti-Semitism that springs from xenophobia than by making this center of European culture himself one of the recognizable "outsiders"? A Jesus who is not obviously one of "those" Jews, who is not a Jew who looks just like "we" expect a Jew to look, cannot serve this purpose. A Jesus who does, however, perform a massive act of inversion and subversion of a sordid European history: a final Christian assimilation and appropriation of the "other"; or the final victory of the "other" by claiming its central place in the culture that repudiated it. In either case—and I am not sure which, if either, is the accurate characterization—the Jewish Jesus of modern scholarship accomplishes, or at least implies, the repositioning of the quintessential outsider as, in fact, in the end, the very center and pinnacle of the dominant culture. "The very stone which the builders rejected has become the head of the corner; this was the Lord's doing, and it is marvelous in our eyes" (Mark 12:10).

The agenda here has two facets. It offers a way to respond to the Holocaust, *and*, simultaneously, a rejoinder to contemporary anti-Semitism. In terms of the former, the travesty of the Holocaust is underscored by insisting on its *irony*. No, the "eternal Jew," as it happens, was not a *threat* to European civilization (and its North American spin-offs), but its *basis*. The Holocaust was thus not only a crime against humanity, but a crime against the very values which were invoked to promote it. Moreover—and it is here that my sympathy with this agenda begins to wane—Jesus the Jew serves as a way to reclaim Christianity from complicity in the Holocaust; even to insulate it from this complicity. Intrinsically, then, Jesus—standing in for the whole of the "true" and "proper" Christian religion[6]—shows that what Christianity is not, at its core, is anti-Jewish or anti-Semitic. How could it be, when its founder was a Jew? And not simply a Jew, but, apparently, a religious and identifiable Jew, a Jew of comparable kind to the Jews who have been so savagely persecuted in the last few centuries by Christians themselves?

The figure of Jesus has often been a device for recasting Christianity, sometimes polemically, in such a way that whatever present features are deemed to be unattractive are eliminated as late accretions, and the "true essence" of Christianity recaptured and revived by appeal to Jesus himself. In short, much Jesus scholarship has just been gospel writing done anew. Is Christianity too dogmatic? It did not used to be; that was a later accretion at the hands of "early catholicism." Is it too supernaturally oriented? Well, Jesus would have no truck with that nonsense. And so, too, was it complicit in centuries upon centuries of inhumanity to Jews, culminating in the "final solution"? Only through the sheerest perversity of those Christians who failed to understand that their religion was created by, and revolves around, the very kind of figure they were abusing. Jesus the Jew, then, stands as the clearest possible indication that Christianity is not anti-Jewish, properly, and so is not implicated in the Holocaust. Christian justifications for and participation in the Nazi movement were perversions—not expressions of what Christianity genuinely and essentially is. Thus Christian anti-Judaism of both the past and present is condemned; thus the responsibility of *contemporary* Christians for the Holocaust is lessened; and thus, especially, are the doors opened to Jewish-Christian interfaith dialogue now that this messy business of anti-Judaism has been dispensed with. This latter point seems to be of special and explicit concern to several authors. Particularly forthright are the comments of Fredriksen and Reinhartz:

> Our hope is that this volume will contribute in positive ways to the efforts of lay readers to understand the historical circumstances of early Christianity. By making this effort, such readers will be able to see how anti-Judaism *entered* Christian theology at a formative stage of its development … determining the church's interpretation of foundational New Testament texts. We also hope this book will help readers to see that we have other interpretive possibilities and available readings when, with historical understanding,

we approach the Christian scriptures. Readings that neither distort history nor encourage prejudice.... As scholars of ancient Christianity *who are committed to interfaith dialogue*, we assemble these essays for you to think with as you study the New Testament. (Fredriksen and Reinhartz 2002, 5, emphasis added)

This particular concern with current Jewish-Christian relations is present, and obvious, throughout a great deal of current New Testament scholarship.

I do not wish to imply that the less-recognizable Jew reconstructed in the historical work of Mack, Crossan, the Jesus Seminar, and so on, is a function of a lack of interest in contemporary anti-Semitism or the Holocaust. Both are critical issues, invested with passion, for all of these scholars. But if so, why do they present us with a Jesus who does not—cannot—stand in for the persecuted, identifiable Jew of modernity? My own hunch is that these scholars recognize that anti-Semitism is more about *ideology* than ancient history; perhaps even more, that historical reconstruction itself is neither the cause nor the cure for anti-Semitism. To put the matter as graphically as possible, what if "the Jews" *were* responsible for the death of Jesus? What if Jesus really *did* call "the Jews" children of the devil (John 8:44)? What if Matthew's words, "his blood be on us and on our children" (Matt 27:25) *were* really, historically, spoken?[7] Would such *historical* conclusions justify the Holocaust? Would they make it a good thing, after all? Would they imply that Christians really should hate Jews? Emphatically, no. Presumably Hitler did not go to war with Churchill, Stalin, and Roosevelt because of their differing historical assessments of Matthew 27:25. The alleged events of the gospels are from the distant past, and, for thinking people today, have, or ought to have, no bearing at all on current interpersonal or inter-religious relations: those must be determined by present attitudes, not obscure historical reconstructions.

And so, it seems to me, the Crossans and Funks of contemporary scholar-ship, in their avoidance of the particular kind of recognizable "religious Jew" promoted by other scholars, are not at all allying themselves with anti-Semitism or approving of the Holocaust; they are, instead, seeking to address anti-Semitism in other ways. We are all, it seems, trying to distance ourselves, politically speaking, from anti-Semitism and its consequences; but the paths taken differ. In the case of scholars such as Crossan and Funk, there *is* an effort to use ancient history to comment on Jewish-Christian relations today. But the history that they focus on is that of characterizations of Jews in the ancient Christian writings. Crossan, that is, goes to great lengths to deny "Jewish" responsibility for the crucifixion; Funk emphatically denies the historicity of Matthew 27:25.

Thus these scholars seem to refrain from taking the final step that I would promote: the recognition that such ancient events in and of themselves, *as* history, are irrelevant to contemporary issues.[8] If they avoid this final step, why would Crossan or Funk not join Sanders, Fredriksen, Chilton, Freyne, and the like in casting Jesus in distinctively "Jewish" garb? I would suggest that at least some of their motivation is precisely to *avoid* the fixed stereotype of "the eternal Jew" used to such great effect by their scholarly rivals. There are always at least two ways to attack stereotypes, especially racial stereotypes. One is to embrace them, reclaim them, and force them to the center of the discourse, as I think may be happening with some "Jewish Jesus" scholarship. Other, contemporary, examples are numerous and obvious: the appropriation, reclamation, and refiguring of words such as "nigger" by blacks, "dyke" by lesbians, and especially all *kinds* of misogynist terminology by Mary Daly (see especially Daly and Caputi 1987). (I am reminded, strangely enough, of Jefferson Airplane's line in the song "We Can be Together" [*Volunteers*, 1969]: "Everything they say we are, we are; and we're very proud of ourselves.") The other response to negative stereotypes, of course, is to deny them emphatically, to show that the hated *image* need not correspond to the reality of actual people and the ways they lead their lives. Thus it seems to me that the contribution of those scholars who give us a "non-Jewish" Jesus is precisely to demonstrate the ways in which *being* a Jew are as multiple and open to possibility as being anything or anyone else. Here the stereotype is attacked by discarding it. In this way, then, both the allegedly "non-Jewish" Jesus and the "Jewish Jesus" advocates are pursuing essentially the same agenda, albeit in different ways.

Burton Mack goes even farther: he quite properly, in my view, rejects the salience of actual historical events (very few of which he regards as residing behind the gospels anyway), and instead associates both anti-Judaism and American triumphalism with contemporary promotions of the gospels' ideologies, particularly that of the Gospel of Mark. The issue here is not whether or how the events recounted in gospel stories intersect with actual historical events; rather, the issue is the overall effect of the story itself on attitudes and conceptions of the self and others. And this, I think, is exactly right. What a small handful of people living in Jerusalem in the year 30 CE or so might have said or done is really of little import; but what is said and implied in canonical writings and in their normative interpretations is of tremendous import. These documents do have a huge impact on contemporary attitudes, precisely because they are canonical. And so Jews today who wish to relate congenially with Christians must somehow address Talmudic slanders against Jesus, just as Christians today must address the much more extensive and dangerous slanders against "the Jews" in their own holy books. As Sanders notes:

> Since the quest of the historical Jesus is recent and academic, we know that its results cannot be crucial to Christianity. The Christ of faith is, of course, crucial, but beliefs about him are not subject to historical investigation ....

> For the most part, Christianity rests on beliefs about God and Christ that cannot conceivably suffer at the rough hands of the historian. (Sanders 2002, 32)

The obvious corollary here is that, ultimately, academic historical conclusions, if they cannot disprove Christian doctrine, cannot improve it either. We may have shifts among many Christians in their understanding of the historical development of their faith, but I would submit that these shifts are a function of theological changes imposing themselves on sacred history; not of an assimilation of academic history to such a point that basic theological beliefs are actually altered. And so, it seems to me, *any* efforts—whether those of Crossan and Funk, or those of their critics—to reconstruct a *history* of Jesus and ancient Christianity that would both serve to separate Christianity from the Holocaust, and to make further Christian anti-Judaism impossible,[9] are doomed to failure because they are addressing the wrong issues. The right issues are attitudes; to be sure, attitudes engendered by the canonical texts of Christianity and by much subsequent Christian theology. But the source of those attitudes is not anything that "the Jews" said or did, nor is it the extent to which Jesus may or may not have agreed with the religious or other cultural practices of his contemporaries. It resides, rather, in the techniques that the emerging Christian religion used, and has continued to use, to define itself over against its parent religion and to maintain its *raison d'être* as a *superior* religion that exists precisely because it expropriated the function of its parent. Until and unless Christianity is able to find a mode of self-definition that does not require a supercessionist theology or a strong contradistinction to Judaism it will never be able to shed its intrinsic tendency to anti-Judaism. We will not—cannot—save Christianity from anti-Semitism, nor assuage our guilt, by making its supposed founder into an honorary Jew.

There remains one final note on the political agenda of the Jewish Jesus construct. I was somewhat amazed to find the following statement in a recent article by Paula Fredriksen, which I must quote here at some length:

> The church had [a] bad year in 1897, on the eve of the first World Zionist Congress: A reconstituted state of Israel, centered around a rebuilt Jerusalem, one Jesuit spokesman averred, was flatly impossible, because it was contrary to the prediction of Christ himself. (I just want to note in passing, if this sort of thing matters to anyone, that the text of Mark 13:2 and parallels says only that all the Temple's stones will be thrown down, not that they will never again be lifted up. The passage was *read*, however, as symbolizing a permanent punishment: That is the point.) For some people 1948, when the state of Israel was established, was another tough year. So, for related reasons, was 1967, when Jerusalem was reunited under Jewish sovereignty. Is anti-Judaism, then, the same as anti-Semitism and anti-Zionism? I do not think so. The first is a theological position; the

second, a racist one; the third, a political one. But, without question, the
long centuries of Christianity's anti-Judaism soaked into the soil of Western
culture, preparing the ground for these more recent avatars. (Fredriksen
2002, 28, emphasis original)

This is a fascinating statement in several respects. First, to hearken back to
my last point about the irrelevance of *fact* over against *interpretation*, I draw
attention to Fredriksen's brief parenthetical discussion of Mark 13:2 and
parallels. First I note, with wholesale approval and delight, her qualification,
"if this sort of thing matters to anyone." Just so. But I also note that while
Fredriksen is, strictly speaking, correct here—neither Mark 13:2 nor its
parallels (Matt 24:2; Luke 21:6) refer to this destruction as permanent—her
comment is also misleading. The synoptists *do* imply that this destruction
will be final: after Jesus predicts the destruction of the temple in these
passages, his disciples ask him when this will occur, and he delivers the
beginnings of a quasi-apocalyptic post-facto description of the Jewish War
(Mark 13:3–20 and parallels). Then, following this, he describes the events
to be associated with his second coming (Mark 13:21–27 and parallels).
It is very clear that Mark, at least, and probably also Matthew and Luke,
believe that the destruction of the temple, and perhaps of Jerusalem itself, is
to remain in effect until the second coming. Luke even says quite explicitly
that "Jerusalem will be trodden down by the Gentiles, until the times of
the Gentiles are fulfilled" (21:24).[10] The Jesuit spokesman Fredriksen refers
to may have been correct in his interpretation of scripture after all. The
reason I mention this is not to be pedantic but to stress again the irrelevance
of such considerations of "correct" biblical interpretation to the unfolding
of history. Fredriksen is quite possibly wrong to imply that the synoptists
are not predicting a final and irrevocable destruction of the temple or re-
establishment of Jerusalem—at least until the apocalypse. *But it does not
matter.* Israel now exists, and a Jewish state controls Jerusalem. Whether or
not Mark or any New Testament texts predicted that this could never be, it
is still the case. Were we to conclude that Mark *did* make such a prediction,
that the Word of God emphatically denies the possibility of Israel, Israel
would still exist. Again, what matters for contemporary political realities
are our own values, opinions, and actions, and not the actual opinions or
actions of those who wrote the New Testament documents, or about whom
these documents were written.

But of even greater interest, to my mind, is Fredriksen's association in
this quotation of the state of Israel, Zionism, and the like, with biblical interpretation. It cannot be doubted, of course, that some Christian opposition
to Zionism has been motivated in part by precisely the factors Fredriksen
documents: a belief that the Bible says it cannot be so, as well as, perhaps,
antipathy toward Jews in general, however motivated.[11] Strangely, though,
the opposite is true as well: many fundamentalist Christians actively support

the state of Israel, not out of any love of the Jewish people, but because of the association I noted above between gospel predictions of the apocalypse and the re-establishment of Jerusalem and/or the temple. That is, some fundamentalist and millenarian-oriented Christians believe that the existence of Israel is a sign of the end times, and so do what they can to support Israel's continued existence, including its contested control over Jerusalem. What seems clear is that both sides of this theological debate do indeed view Israel's existence as a matter impacting on religious belief, and especially on beliefs based on interpretation of the New Testament gospels. Thus, it appears to me, Fredriksen's comments acknowledge her awareness of this strange fact, and suggest an agenda of her own in this debate: to reconstruct a history of ancient Christianity amenable to an interpretation of these texts supporting the continued existence of the state of Israel, but which, *unlike* the views of Christian fundamentalists, supports this state as having legitimate claims in its own right.

What Fredriksen is suggesting, then, is that the anti-Judaic interpretive schema of later, Gentile, Christianity is responsible for a misreading of originary and/or canonical texts in such a way as to suggest the illegitimacy or impossibility of the existence of modern Israel (Fredriksen 2002, 27–29). That existence and possibility is then "defended" by a reinterpretation of both Christian texts and originary events as emanating from a *Jewish* environment, and so undercutting the validity of anti-Jewish interpretations thereof, including, of course, those that oppose Zionism. In this way, the Jewish Jesus himself can become—and I suspect is, in the minds of at least some scholars (and their readers)—a symbolic justification for the state of Israel. This may seem like quite a stretch, but we are not talking here, for the most part, about logical and direct arguments, but instead about symbols, attitudes, and general ideological suggestions. In the work of scholars such as Sanders, Freyne, Fredriksen, Meier, and Chilton, we have a Jesus who is not only Jewish, but who—unlike the *Galilean* Jesuses of Horsley, Mack, or Crossan—concerns himself with the Temple cultus and not only shows an affinity to Judean Judaism but is actively engaged with it in Jerusalem itself. In the case of Freyne, too, a strong emphasis is placed on the (putative) Galilean concern, hence presumably shared by Jesus, with the land of Israel as a holy land. Such a Jesus can serve as a potent demonstration of the positive value and enduring import of a Jewish Jerusalem and a Jewish Israel. At the very least, the picture of a truly Jewish Jerusalem is presented to the readers of such scholarship; at the most, a claim is being offered that the (supposedly) most important figure of western history strongly associated his (Jewish) religion with this holy city. Such a presentation can only serve to strengthen the legitimacy of Israel as a Jewish state, and especially its claims to the city of Jerusalem.

Religious Identities

Of course, the figure of Jesus is also important precisely because of his *religious* centrality; he was never a political leader, or a military general, or any such thing, but is imagined to have founded a religion. We should expect, then, that the manufactured debate over the "Jewish Jesus" should reflect religious anxieties and agenda as well. Again, I want to stress that since no one in contemporary scholarship *denies* that Jesus was a Jew, the debated issue is really *what kind* of Jew he was. In effect, then, the rhetoric sometimes being employed—better scholars produce a Jewish Jesus, while inferior scholars produce a non-Jewish Jesus—suggests that there are certain ways of behaving that *make* one non-Jewish, that *exclude* one from Jewish identity. In short, what we have here is a construction of and debate about what constitutes a "true" Jew.

Of all of the covert agenda behind this discussion, this one is probably the most clear. Of course, the stage onto which it is projected is antiquity, not the present, and so advocates of the peculiarly reified and rigidly Jewish Jesus can deny the applicability of their dismissals to the present and to questions of Jewish identity today. But the fact is that critics such as Pearson, Hays, Meier, and Sanders are claiming that some modern scholars are producing a non-Jewish Jesus even when those scholars specifically assert that their Jesuses *are* Jewish; and scholars such as Fredriksen, Chilton, and Wright feel fairly confident in making inferences from the fact of Jesus' Judaism to the character of his behavior and teaching. What this implies is that all of these scholars have a clear idea of what "Judaism," as a religious entity, *must* be, and are using that idea as a template for reconstructing who Jesus, therefore, *must have* (or must not have) been. In short, we are here in the presence of a *normative* definition of Judaism.

The "real" form of Judaism that is being advocated here is, as I noted above, one that tends to have significant affinities with certain forms of contemporary, albeit traditional, Judaism. In the Judaism of the Jewish Jesus, there tends to be a focus on Torah, the interpretation thereof and obedience thereto. The temple figures significantly, as does, at times, eschatological expectation. So too does concern with the holy land of God's promise, Israel, and the native Semitic speech of the inhabitants. Jesus is a rabbi and debates with rabbis; he is attendant at festivals and honors the Sabbath; he is circumcised.

The question that arises here is precisely why, if indeed, this construction of Judaism is intended to be normative, any of these scholars would care at all about the current construction of the Jewish religion, especially since very few of them are themselves Jewish. As Marianne Sawicki incisively notes:

> How can a meaningful Jewish identity today and tomorrow be secured
> through claiming certain people, places, and practices of the past as

the antecedents and sources of one's own Jewishness? This question I respectfully leave for Jews to address; a Christian has no business trying to tell Jews how to be who they are. (Sawicki 2000, 232)

Without actually knowing anything about which historical Jesus scholars might themselves be religious Jews, if any, I can nonetheless surmise that the reconstructions of ancient Judaism, and Jesus with them, that employ the normative definition discussed above may very well, as Sawicki implies, be offered in the service of "claiming certain people, places, and practices of the past as the antecedents and sources of one's own Jewishness." Such claims not only may serve a particular "insider" construction of contemporary Judaism, but, additionally, serve the purposes of intra-Jewish polemic, particularly useful against Reform Judaism. This last possibility would not even have occurred to me had Rodney Stark not suggested an explicit comparison between the marginalized Diaspora Judaism of antiquity and that of modern Europe. Stark claims:

> *People will attempt to escape or resolve a marginal position.* Some Jews in the nineteenth century tried to resolve their marginality by assimilation, including conversion to Christianity. Others attempted to resolve their marginality by becoming a new kind of Jew. Reform Judaism was designed to provide a nontribal, non-ethnic [sic] religion rooted in the Old Testament (and the Enlightenment), one that focused on theology and ethics rather than custom and practice…. [It] is forthright in its attempt to strip ethnicity from theology. (Stark 1996, 52–53; emphasis original)

Stark is no historical Jesus scholar, and there is reason enough to doubt his reconstruction of an earliest Christianity marked by large-scale "conversion" of Jews. But his comments here must draw our attention to the ways in which a denial of the Jewish character of the figure reconstructed by Crossan, or Mack, or the Jesus Seminar, implies with it a denial of the Jewish character of modern Reform Judaism. If Crossan's Jesus is no Jew, then neither was, say, Rabbi Samuel Holdheim, the first Rabbi of Berlin's Reform congregation. Such a conclusion would, of course, be very congenial to many religious Jews, who may indeed hold that, religiously speaking, Reform Judaism is no Judaism at all. Of course, I must stress again that I honestly do not know which, if *any*, of the "Jewish Jesus" advocates are themselves Jewish or would for any reason be interested in such a campaign. But I cannot help but feel that, at the very least, the polemics of scholars such as Sanders, Meier, Pearson, and Hays are congenial in their implication that there is essentially *one* way of being Jewish, and that those who fail to adhere to that narrow path are, simply, not Jewish at all.

One might additionally surmise that those Christian and other non-Jewish scholars (who constitute the majority in this field, I am certain) who are constructing such a rigid and fixed image of ancient Judaism are simply projecting onto antiquity their own beliefs about the key hallmarks of Judaism, and are reluctant enough to let go of these presumptions that they criticize any Jesus who does not conform to them as "un-Jewish." But I think much more is at issue here than simple fixed ideas about Judaism as a religion. Again, I would insist that a normative and prescriptive agenda lurks behind these characterizations, such that a claim is being made that a person who fails to accord to these (or similar) criteria is not simply unidentifiable as a religious Jew, but, whatever protestations to the contrary, is actually *not* a (proper) religious Jew.

As Sawicki reminds us, the Christian, or any other non-Jew, has no business telling Jews what they ought to believe and do, nor has any business at all in defining their religious traditions in any normative respect (scholarly efforts at *analytic* classification are, of course, a different matter). But it would not strike me as especially surprising, in light of the hubris of Christianity and its influence on those raised in its shadows, for Christians to do just this. After all, it must surely strike one as odd that all of the supposed definitional hallmarks of ancient Judaism are precisely the features that have been invoked in traditional anti-Jewish Christian polemic. Temple, Torah, the land of Israel, ethnic identity, circumcision—are these not precisely the features that Christians, historically, have grasped as the salient points of their distinction from Judaism? Should we not then worry that some Christian scholars are insisting on such an identity for Judaism precisely so that a distinctive Christian identity can be maintained? After all, if Jesus the Jew turns out to be defined mainly in terms of such things as, say, belief in God, interest in the prophetic scriptures, interest in ethical behavior, the prioritization of love of one's neighbor and one's personal duty over against the strictures of custom, and so on, then might it not turn out that Judaism could and can include and embrace everything that Christianity claims to be? And if so, why bother to be a Christian at all? So it seems to me that, perhaps, Christians, or Gentiles from a Christian background that may still mean something to them, do indeed have a vested interest in defining a normative Judaism, in order to define themselves.

But there is more still. The character of the Judaism imposed, as a discrete and fixed system, upon the figure of Jesus is one marked above all by its traditionalism and by claims to a common and rather standardized conformity to key distinctive behaviors and doctrines. This is necessarily a common feature of the Jewish Jesus reconstructions, since these reconstructions depend on a stable image of Judaism from which to make inferences about Jesus. It is essentially impossible to reconstruct a fluid, non-conformist, variegated Judaism from which to make inferences about Jesus' "religiosity" for the simple reason that one would not know where, amidst this variety, to slot Jesus. The specific content of these fixed behaviors and doctrines, in at least one sense, hardly matters. What may be of more importance to non-Jews, and particularly Christians, is the *identification* of a particular religion with the "fundamentals," the observance of and adherence to its *traditional* identity. If, for instance, "Jesus the Cynic"[12] can be no Jew, this implies that such a syncretistic, assimilatory, socially engaged, or radical option can exist in *no* religious tradition; that, properly speaking, such traditions are and must be focused on their "proper" objects, and to the extent that their adherents are *not* so oriented, they are no longer a part of the tradition to which they lay claim.

While I imagine that the main interest of those promoting such a view rests with Christianity (and Judaism to a more limited degree), the basic point can apply to just about any modern religion. Thus by identifying "Jesus the Jew" as only conceivably meaning "Jesus the Torah-observant, Semitic-speaking, circumcised, Temple-oriented, Sabbath-observant Jew" one speaks, again normatively, for a whole host of other traditions, and, more perniciously, *against* a whole host of contemporary religious options hanging by their fingernails at the peripheries of their traditions. If, for instance, Pearson is correct that Crossan's characterization of Jesus as a Jewish Cynic is an oxymoron (so Pearson 1996, 12, referring to Crossan 1991, 421), then we should similarly dismiss as oxymoronic such phenomena as Marxist Catholic priests, feminist Muslims, atheistic Zionists, homosexual Cree traditionalists, Communist Taoists, and so on. Of course, such phenomena *do* exist; wishing them out of existence is not the point. The world is a messy place. The point, rather, is denying them the legitimating links to the traditions they lay claim to. Feminist Muslims, for instance, may be decried by their opponents as no Muslims at all (see, e.g., Khan 2002); in short, they are an oxymoron. A traditionalist view of Islam has no place for such an agenda at all, and so its proponents are cast outside of the tradition. Thus too, by offering up a definition of the boundaries of Judaism that exclude all but a traditionalist perspective from genuine belonging in the religion, the more rigid "Jewish Jesus" scholars may be suggesting a similarly traditionalist definition of Christianity: not a fundamentalist definition, necessarily, but one in which assent to the creeds, belief in God, veneration for God's word in the canonical Bible, and the general supernatural paraphernalia of orthodox Christian faith are the litmus test for whether one can, or cannot, claim to be a Christian at all.

Confirmation that this retrenchment of traditionalist Christian identity may be a subtext for at least some historical Jesus scholars may be found in an odd and interesting place: the theological agenda of their opponents. New Testament scholars such as John Dominic Crossan and Robert Funk make no secret at all of their interest in *reforming* a Christianity to which they are in some fashion committed. And for both of these scholars, and others besides (e.g., Marcus Borg, Stephen Patterson, and many of the participants in the Jesus Seminar), this reform is oriented especially to a marginalization of the purely supernatural and dogmatic orientation of the religion, and an emphasis instead on its social and cultural effects. The Jesus of a Crossan or Funk is a Jesus who is quite clearly intended to inspire Christian followers of Jesus to become more engaged in this world, more socially active, and less rigid about or even concerned with dogmatic or credal formulations. Funk, for instance, compares his own project with that of Galileo, shunting aside the gloomy clouds of dogma to free us from their slavery and open us to the truth (Funk and Hoover 1993, 1–4). So also Crossan, who reconstructs a Jesus who promoted "a religious and economic egalitarianism that negated alike and at once the hierarchical and patronal normalcies of Jewish religion and Roman power" (Crossan 1991, 422). And lest we miss the ultimate import of these ciphers—"normalcies of Jewish religion" as conservative Christianity and "Roman power" as especially American military hegemony over the world—Crossan introduces a contemporizing figure or two to his discussion. This Jesus who promoted the egalitarianism described by Crossan can be interpreted in terms of the Cynics, who "were hippies in a world of Augustan yuppies" (Crossan 1991, 421). Crossan's comments on apocalypticism, while they do not directly reflect on the "Jewish" character of the historical Jesus, also show us something about Crossan's religious orientation and agenda:

> We are guilty of historical malpractice to go on using a phrase that can only misunderstand the past and *mislead the present. A millenarian seer or apocalyptic prophet announces the imminent transcendental change of a terribly evil world into a perfectly good one.* Say that clearly, and we might get somewhere. At least we might get to something *worth arguing about.* Go on talking about "the end of the world" and only misunderstanding and *irrelevance* are possible. (Crossan, in Miller 2001, 138; some emphasis added)

Moreover, says Crossan, historical reconstruction is at the very heart of Christianity (Crossan 1991, 423–26), and he laments that:

> Maybe, Christianity is an inevitable and absolutely necessary "betrayal" of Jesus, else it might have died among the hills of Lower Galilee. But did that "betrayal" have to happen so swiftly, succeed so fully, and be enjoyed so thoroughly? Might not a more even dialectic have been maintained between Jesus and Christ in Jesus Christ? (Crossan 1991, 424)

Crossan, as much as Funk and much more clearly, is at least partly interested in a historical Jesus who will serve as a reforming model for modern Christianity, moving it away from a dogmatic focus and more toward a socially activist focus. Hence a reconstruction of Jesus who is not defined in terms of Jewish religiosity (which remains an anachronistic distinction) is a Jesus who offers a model for a type of Christianity that maintains its relevance in a secular world.

This last point is especially worth stressing. I do not suspect that either Funk's or Crossan's agenda is precisely to *secularize* Christianity simply because of some alleged desire to promote secularism (against Pearson 1996, 42–43). Rather I suspect that, especially in the case of Crossan, the ultimate agenda is to *preserve* a place for Christianity within a world in which, say, the doctrine of Trinity or the rituals of the Mass appear to have less and less relevance. The situation is quite different for Burton Mack, however. Here the agenda seems not only to be genuinely secularizing, but even anti-Christian (at least in its American forms). The last chapter of *A Myth of Innocence* makes it very clear that Mack believes that Christianity has, historically, had an undesirable (to say the least) impact on our attitudes and behaviors. And so I suspect that at least in part the "non-religious" (and hence, for those who are using "Jewish" as a cipher for "religious," the "non-Jewish") Jesus he constructs is intended to serve as a *poor,* even *impossible,* basis for contemporary self-understanding and social practice.

In any case, regardless of the ultimate motivations of Funk, Crossan, Mack, or others, I am suggesting that behind their lack of emphasis on the specifically *religious* features of Jesus' teaching and activity is neither an anti-Semitism nor an anti-Judaism, but a desire to minimize the doctrinal, credal, and supernaturalistic elements of Christianity. To my mind this serves as further indication that those who do precisely the opposite—i.e., who stress the "Judaism" of Jesus by stressing the "religious" dimensions of his thought or actions—are likewise making a comment on contemporary Christianity, an assertion of the import of its traditional credal, supernatural, "religious" basis. Pearson's fulminations against the "secular" Jesus reconstructed by the Jesus Seminar underscore and confirm this conclusion:

> The "hidden agenda" in the work of the Jesus Seminar is clearly an ideology that drives it. So what is this ideology? An important clue is found in the frequency with which the word "secular" appears in *The Five Gospels*…. The ideology driving the Jesus Seminar is, I would argue, one of "secularization." … What we have … is an approach driven by an ideology of secularization, and a process of coloring the historical evidence to fit a secular ideal. Thus, in robbing Jesus of his Jewishness, the Jesus Seminar has finally robbed him of his *religion*. (Pearson 1996, 42–43; emphasis original)

I do not offer this quotation as further evidence of a secularizing undercurrent behind the Jesus Seminar, but as evidence that that accusation that their (and others') reconstruction of Jesus is non-Jewish itself betrays the undercurrent of an *anti*-secularizing perception of religion. It is not that Pearson, or any of the critics of the Jesus Seminar, necessarily think that Canada or the United States should be theocracies, of course. It is that they wish, apparently, to use Jesus as a model for insisting on traditional perceptions of religion and what it means to be religious. Thus, as noted, "Jesus the Jew" may be offered in the service of such a prescriptive, normative understanding of religion. Indeed, Pearson himself links the two in the quotation above.

Pearson also, interestingly, accuses the Jesus Seminar of an "obvious anachronism" in their use of the term "secular" (Pearson 1996, 43), and yet in the same paragraph claims that they have robbed Jesus of his *religion*! While I must offer a qualified assent to the claim that "secular" is an anachronism in this context, such a claim *must* imply that "religion" is equally anachronistic. This point seems to be one that many people have a hard time understanding, for reasons that baffle me, so I feel the need to explain here precisely what I mean. Pearson's claim that "secular" is an anachronism as applied to antiquity clearly *cannot* mean that those things we today tend to identify as secular— say, paying taxes or drinking beer—did not actually exist in antiquity. Such a claim is false and obviously so. Rather, Pearson's claim is based on the *correct* perception that our classification of such things as secular does not apply to antiquity: the ancients did not typically distinguish or categorize things this way. But "secular," in the sense being used in *The Five Gospels* (Funk, Hoover, and the Jesus Seminar 1993), means nothing more than "not religious." Hence the assertion that identifying anything in antiquity as "secular" is anachronistic implies (again, correctly; see Arnal 2000a, 2001b; Asad 1993) that this is because the ancients did not differentiate the "religious" from anything else. This then requires the conclusion that either *everything* in antiquity was, or potentially was, "religious," or that *nothing* was "religious" in any meaningful way. In either case, by rejecting the classification "secular" as anachronistic, Pearson logically precludes himself from invoking "religion."

Note too that these conclusions must be qualified as they apply to actual scholarly writing. When a scholar, such as Vermès, refers to the "religion of Jesus" he is indeed guilty of an anachronism, strictly speaking. But we do, today, operate in terms of "religion" as a valid classification, and so it seems to me perfectly appropriate to bring together certain aspects of antiquity that are related to each other by *our* conceptions, not those of the ancients themselves (on which see also Smith 1982a, xi–xii). Thus if I am interested in beliefs and activities that I, as a modern, would classify as religious, there is no particular reason *not* to lump these together and analyze how they were treated in a culture—say, ancient Babylonia—in which they were *not* lumped together. Hence trying to reconstruct, for instance, "the politics of Jesus" is perfectly legitimate even though Jesus, presumably, would not have set these particular views aside as "political." But scholars who do this should recognize that these classificatory schemata are their own, not those of the persons they analyze, and so should very rigorously refrain from drawing *any* conclusions that assume, for instance, the *emic* systematicity or unity of such classes of practices. This, in addition to his self-contradiction, is precisely what Pearson is guilty of: he has misunderstood both the Jesus Seminar (which, it seems to me, was using "secular" in the sense of "what we moderns would consider secular") and antiquity (which, if it could not identify an object as "secular," could neither identify it as "religious"; or, to put it another way, if *anything* can be religious, a Jesus who does *anything* can never be "robbed of his religion").

Pearson is not just trying to eat his cake and have it too, he is trying to eat a cake that he himself recognizes does not exist. Such obvious illogic must indicate that purely academic issues are not being debated here; something very important is at stake. Since I know nothing about Pearson's own religious views (or lack thereof), it is impossible for me to say that he is actively promoting desecularization here. In fact, I very much doubt that this is the case, since Pearson quite explicitly defends non-theological approaches to historical scholarship (1996, 43): "Of course, one should expect that, in secular academic settings (such as a state university in the U.S.), a non-theological approach to historical evidence, including religious evidence, is standard. In my view, it ought to be the starting point even for theological historical research." But what he is resisting is the secularization of *religion*: the figure of Jesus cannot be "secular," for this would imply a definition of Christianity (or, in theory, any other religious tradition: Judaism, Islam, Buddhism, etc.) quite at odds with its traditional self-presentation.

Finally, an additional piece of evidence that the Jewish Jesus "debate" is the manifest content of a latent engagement (positive or negative) with traditionalistic definitions of religion (usually, though not necessarily, Christianity) may be found in the differing treatment of each "camp" in the debate over extra-canonical sources. This is most marked in the case of the *Gospel of Thomas*, and the differing assessments of its utility for historical Jesus research. Typically, those scholars who actively promote the traditionalistic and identifiable Jewish religiosity of the historical Jesus explicitly reject the *Gospel of Thomas* as having any utility for historical Jesus work, or simply ignore it as a potential source. For example, John Meier offers explicit arguments for rejecting *Thomas* in volume 1 of *Marginal Jew* (1991), though these arguments are weak, reversible, or assume their conclusions. Fredriksen mentions *Thomas* only twice in *Jesus of Nazareth* (1999, 81, 269), describing it in both instances as "late." Vermès refers to *Thomas* just once (1993, 82), asserting without argument that saying #31 is literarily dependent on the synoptic gospels. Pearson criticizes the Jesus Seminar for using *Thomas*, for the usual variety of reasons, but additionally criticizes them for positing an early edition of *Thomas*. He states, "No convincing case can be made … for an early 'first edition' of the *Gospel of Thomas*" (Pearson 1996, 15). It is interesting that here Pearson says no such case *can* be made, not that no such case *has* been made: the idea is simply impossible as far as he is concerned. In fact arguments *have* been made for the existence of an early stratum of *Thomas* (convincing or not) by a variety of scholars, including extended arguments on this issue by myself (Arnal 1995) and more recently by April De Conick (De Conick 2002). Conversely, those scholars who tend to be accused of producing a "non-Jewish" Jesus—Crossan, Mack, the Jesus Seminar, and so on—*do* tend to make use of *Thomas* in their reconstructions of Jesus.

Here is not the place to engage the debate about *Thomas*'s date or dependence on the synoptic gospels.[13] But it is worth noting two peculiar features of the debate about *Thomas*'s applicability to historical Jesus research. The first is that those who offer reasons for rejecting *Thomas* as a source tend to do so on three grounds: (1) it is a late document; (2) it is dependent on one or more of the synoptic gospels; (3) it is Gnostic in its theological orientation (e.g., Meier 1991, 112–41; Pearson 1996, 15; and many others). What is interesting about this set of arguments is that *even if* all three of these assertions were accurate, that would still provide no logical reason whatsoever for rejecting *Thomas*'s applicability to historical Jesus research. As it happens, the exact same types of arguments indisputably apply to the gospels of Matthew and Luke (in contrast to *Thomas*, in fact, where all three points are in dispute): (1) they are late compositions, ranging in date somewhere between 85–120 CE; (2) they are dependent on other synoptic sources (Mark and Q); (3) they promote their own distinctive theologies. Yet those scholars who reject *Thomas* on these grounds are happy enough to mine Matthew and Luke for potentially "authentic" Jesus material, and rightly so, since being late, or dependent, or theologically biased hardly *precludes* the presence of earlier, authentic material that could not have been gleaned from other sources. The classic example here is the parable of the Good Samaritan (Luke 10:29–37). This parable is generally thought to go back to the historical Jesus in some form (without its Lukan applicative clauses), even though (1) it is singly-attested, (2) in a late (possibly second-century) source, (3) which is dependent on Mark and Q, and (4) which uses the parable to promote the author's own theological-ethical agenda. It would seem, then, that the reasons given for rejecting *Thomas*'s utility are duplicitous, since these arguments are applied selectively. When such claims can be made about non-canonical writings, those potential sources are set aside as irrelevant. When such claims can be made about canonical sources, by contrast, they are made in the service of methodological rigor, rather than wholesale dismissal. Thus, again, the *reasons* given for the repudiation of *Thomas* as a source for the historical Jesus demonstrate a lack of consistency, a duplicity, in the treatment of canonical over against non-canonical sources.

The second peculiar feature of this debate is precisely the co-ordination between the use of *Thomas* as a source and the scholarship that allegedly produces a "non-Jewish" Jesus. This is peculiar precisely because *Thomas* is no less "Jewish" than the synoptic Gospels. In other words, were *Thomas* to offer us a genuinely non-Jewish Jesus, were it to show no concern with the "religious" features of ancient Judaism, were it to address Gentile concerns or presume a Gentile audience, then its use as a source for reconstructing Jesus would quite naturally and comprehensibly co-ordinate with changes of a "non-Jewish" Jesus.[14] Likewise, were the Gospel of Mark to promote the "religious" features of ancient Judaism, were it to stress the Judaism of Jesus, and to take a Jewish audience for granted, then its use as the primary source of information among "Jewish Jesus" advocates would make perfect sense: the tendencies of the reconstructions would reflect the character of the sources used.[15]

But this does not seem to be the case. Mark does not actually give us a Jesus who positively interacts with the supposed features of the "common Judaism" of his time. It is Mark who has Jesus abrogate dietary laws wholesale (7:14–19) and variously violate the Sabbath (especially Mark 2:23–28[16]), who feels the need to explain (incorrectly—so, e.g., Levine 2002, 81) the purification practices of "all the Jews" in the third person (7:3–4), and who ultimately lays responsibility (and, arguably, divine vengeance) for Jesus' death at the feet of the Jewish religious leaders and even the whole crowd present in Jerusalem for the Passover festival.[17] Conversely, it is the *Gospel of Thomas* that insists, against Mark's version of Jesus, on the necessity of both fasting and Sabbath observance: "If you do not fast as regards the world, you will not find the Kingdom. If you do not observe the Sabbath as a Sabbath, you will not see the Father" (#27). *Thomas*, rather than disparaging Jesus' family as Mark does (Mark 3:21, 31–35), asserts the leadership and centrality of his brother James the righteous (#12), traditionally presented as a nomistic rigorist (cf. Gal 2:12). *Thomas* alludes to or quotes Hebrew scriptures (see saying #66, quoting Ps 118:22–23; and saying #17, which may allude to Isa 64:4 and 65:17), uses (albeit inconsistently) the pious Jewish locution "kingdom of heaven" (see, e.g., saying #20), assumes that the Pharisees and scribes possess the "keys of knowledge" (#39), discusses angels and prophets (#88), and takes it for granted that his readers' history is Jewish history (see, e.g., saying #46: "from Adam to John the Baptist"). He offers an interpretation of the parable of the tenants that, unlike Mark's, is not anti-Jewish at all,[18] and an interpretation of the parable of the banquet that, unlike Matthew's or Luke's, has nothing to do with promoting or justifying a Gentile mission.[19]

My point is not that the *Gospel of Thomas* is a "Jewish" text and Mark is not. There are many places in Mark, obviously, where scripture is cited, where the importance of Jewish "religious" practices are emphasized or taken for granted, and the action quite clearly takes place, for the most part, among Jews. So too there are instances in the *Gospel of Thomas* of the sorts of "non-Jewish" or "anti-Jewish" features noted in Mark. *Thomas* saying

#14, for instance, denigrates fasting, prayer, and almsgiving, and appears to dismiss dietary regulations; saying #43 refers to "the Jews" in the third person and seems to assume a distinction between them and Jesus' disciples; and saying #53 implies that circumcision is useless. My point, however, is that neither Mark nor *Thomas* are consistently "Jewish" or "non-Jewish." In short, while there is a very strong correspondence between the rejection of *Thomas* as a source (on inconsistent grounds) and the construction of a traditionalistic "Jewish Jesus," this correspondence cannot be traced to *Thomas*'s actual content, which gives us no more nor less "Jewish" a Jesus than Mark does.

The correspondence, therefore, must be the result of some other factors than the actual contents of the sources in question. I suggest, then, that the clear rejection of *Thomas* as a source for Jesus by "Jewish Jesus" advocates, and the rejection of reconstructions of Jesus that do make use of *Thomas*, confirms my claims above about at least part of the agenda behind this scholarship and the manufactured "debate" over Jesus' Jewishness. That agenda appears at least in part to revolve around the retrenchment of traditionalist religious identity, particularly Christian identity. A Jesus who can *be* a Jew *only* by being an identifiably religiously-focused Jew of a certain traditionalistic sort of course implies a particular vision of religious identity. A Jesus who does not conform to this stereotype implies an opposite vision of religious identity. And so also with the treatment of canonical versus non-canonical documents as sources for Jesus. Although there is no logical relationship between a "Jewish Jesus" and eschewing the *Gospel of Thomas* as a source, the two positions are clearly correlated; they are correlated, I submit, by their common subtext. For those whose vision or imagination of what Christianity *is*, is as it is defined by its traditional adherents, the notion that non-canonical, "heretical" sources might be accurate or should even be given consideration is as unattractive, even unthinkable, as is a "secular" Jesus. And again, the reverse is true. Those scholars who, for whatever personal reasons, wish to open the boundaries of Christianity to secular, reformist, or non-traditional alterations are consistently inclined to be liberal in their use of sources as well. This tendency is especially marked in the work of Crossan, who not only uses *Thomas* as a source, but also appeals to, *inter alia*, the Egerton Gospel and the "Cross Gospel" as early and valuable texts. The problem, then, may not be that *Thomas*'s contents are inimical to either traditional Christian theological views or traditional historical reconstructions (though this may be a factor too: see Kloppenborg Verbin 2000b, 2: "Q— along with the Gospel of Thomas, the epistle of James, and the *Gospel of Peter*—lets us see that the process that led to the formation of the Gospels was incomparably richer, more complex, and more experimental than earlier models have supposed"). Rather, *Thomas* is to be rejected regardless of its contents or their implications (the interpretation of which remain under dispute) simply because it is not canonical. Since *Thomas* is not part of the traditional construction of the Christian religion, it cannot be part of the historical *re*construction of a traditionalist Christianity. Should anyone doubt this claim, I invite them to consider Meier's "argument" in the first volume of *A Marginal Jew* on the value of non-canonical sources (1991, 112–41). Not only are Meier's arguments on the secondary character of *Thomas* logically worthless—more to the point, he argues that having dispensed with a small number of non-canonical sources, this should put to rest any notion that non-canonical sources in general and as a whole may be of any utility to the historical Jesus quest. One could ask for no clearer evidence that Meier, at least, is thinking in terms of two classes of objects—canonical and non-canonical texts—rather than in terms of a multiplicity of discrete and individual texts. In other words, he is clearly assessing the value of his sources *in terms of* canonicity, rather than in terms of the actual evidence. Thus those who depend on "Jesus the Jew" to support traditionalistic reconstructions also reject *Thomas*, even though the use of *Thomas* need not lead to a "non-Jewish" Jesus; and those whose agenda of reform, broadening, or some form of "secularization" generates the accusation of a "non-Jewish" Jesus tend to make some use of *Thomas* and other non-canonical sources, not because these sources are more "secular" than the canonical gospels, but precisely because these scholars are not wedded to the traditional Christian canon.

It would seem, then, that for some contemporary scholars, Christianity (or any "religion") in a secular world will maintain its identity by keeping a tight hold upon its dogmatic roots, its traditional boundaries, its distinctively *religious* nature, as opposed to and autonomous from the secular world around it. For other scholars, Christianity (or any "religion") in a secular world can only be saved by accommodation to that secularity, an assertion of the socio-cultural relevance of Christianity as something larger than mere dogma and worship. This agenda impacts not only on how Jesus is constructed, but also seems to determine what sources are allowable—regardless of the actual *content* of those sources. It is important to note here, in passing, that the significance of this particular subtext cannot be measured wholly in terms of the personal agenda or beliefs of the scholars in question themselves. In some cases, of course, it can be so measured, and quite easily. That scholars such as Pearson or Meier—never mind apologetes such as Wright—have something of a religious agenda of their own that revolves around a traditional understanding of the identity of Christianity is quite obvious (by "traditional," I do not mean necessarily politically conservative or "fundamentalist"). Likewise, with scholars such as Crossan, Funk, or Patterson, it is fairly clear that there is a personal investment in Christianity, but that the Christianity in question is felt to require reform, including reform of its actual identity. With other scholars, however, the situation is not nearly so clear. On the "Jewish Jesus" side of the "debate," scholars such as Fredriksen or Sanders do *not* make it clear (at least not to me) what personal religious commitments they may have, if any, and of what sort those commitments might be. On the other side of the "debate," it is unclear to me what interest Richard Horsley has in contemporary Christianity, and while Burton Mack's agenda is fairly clear, it certainly cannot be described as a *theological* agenda.

But, in at least one sense, the question of *personal* agenda is irrelevant. As I hope I have shown, there is a *correspondence* between the "Jewish Jesus" and a (subtextual) defense of traditionalistic understandings of discrete religions. This correspondence is what is important; not the personal beliefs of individual scholars. There need not be a notion here of direct cause and effect. That is, one need not say that the subtext *causes* the particular characteristics of the historical reconstruction. They just go together, and the one stands in for or supports the other. The subtexts may, however, explain the *heat* generated in a "debate" over Jesus' Judaism in which no one denies that he is Jewish. The anger, recriminations, and misrepresentations derive their energy from the subtexts that each type of reconstruction supports. In addition, these subtexts also have a determining effect on the *reception* of this scholarship. So, regardless of, say, Sanders's personal religious beliefs, traditionalistic Christians will tend to approve of his version of the historical Jesus much more than they will of, say, Crossan's; while Christians who are alienated with or distressed about their religious tradition will tend to find Crossan much more helpful and illuminating than Sanders.

Should anyone doubt this conclusion, I suggest they consult www. amazon.com (or similar sites) and browse through the reader reviews of books by Crossan, the Jesus Seminar, and the like, on the one hand; and those of Fredriksen or Sanders, on the other. They will find there much more straightforwardly religious-based fulminations against Funk or Crossan, and much more general approval—from those coming from an obviously Christian, but not fundamentalist, perspective—for Sanders or Fredriksen. For instance, regarding Sanders's *Historical Figure of Jesus* (Sanders 1993), we find the following reader assessment: "The important point for me is that this excellent historical study of Jesus will not undermine the faith (beliefs), in the slightest, [of] any practicing Christian." Conversely, for Crossan's *Jesus, a Revolutionary Biography*, we get:

> This book, even to an amateur student of the historicity and reliability of the gospels' account of Jesus, is utterly ridiculous. Crossan works from the perspective that what the Bible says must be wrong, and tries to fit all his evidence to fit that perspective. Relying on a number of historical documents that date much later than the gospels themselves is awfully bias [*sic*] for a supposedly objective scholar.

Clearer still is the following rejoinder to Crossan:

> In summation, this book adds up to ... not much. The Jesus presented here would be unrecognizable to believers throughout history, including those who walked with him while he was on this earth. In attempting to make Jesus "relevant" to a politically-correct post-modern world, Crossan strips him of all his uniqueness and presents him as a powerless figure unworthy of worship or following in any religious or spiritual sense. This picture of Jesus is like a jigsaw puzzle with 95% of the pieces missing.

There can be little doubt that the historical Jesus, as has always been the case, is being invoked as a cipher for religious identity.

Cultural Identities

The final subtextual matter I wish to address concerns the ways in which reconstructions of the historical Jesus as a particular type of Jew can be correlated to a cultural malaise of our own time, a malaise that sometimes is expressed by the tag "postmodernism." Too often, "postmodernism" is understood to be an epistemological conclusion that boils down to little more than hermeneutical relativism (e.g. Moore 1989). As anyone should realize, however, philosophical relativism is an old, old viewpoint, and we hardly needed "postmodernism" to introduce us to it. The term "postmodernism" originally appears to have arisen in connection with *architecture*: it described a building style fiercely at odds with the high-modern styles that generated those appalling high-rise housing projects that mar the surface of large cities today. Postmodernist architecture rejected the values of uniformity, functionality, aesthetic coherence, and geometric precision, preferring instead frivolity, mixtures of styles (often jarring), quotation,[20] ornamentality, and geometric anarchy. This architectural style and the values behind it very quickly spread to other areas of culture: literature, art, film, and academic work (for a thorough discussion, see Jameson 1991).

The best explanation for this flood of distinctively postmodern cultural preferences has been an appeal to a postmodern *condition*, which is socially, politically, and/or economically distinctive enough from high-modernity and its expectations that it has generated its own distinctive cultural forms of expression as well (Harvey 1989; cf. Arnal 2001b). The conditions of postmodernity are ones under which we *all* live, and so in some sense any and every reconstruction of the historical Jesus is "postmodern." Crossan may be accused of having produced a "postmodern" Jesus, but the alternatives to his Jesus, no matter how different they may be, are also being generated out of a postmodern context.[21] And what is this postmodern condition? It is to be found, primarily, in the corrosion of social and political categories, as its cultural expressions would imply in *their* corrosion of taken-for-granted categories. Much more recently, this condition has come to be referred to as "globalization."[22] Since the 1970s, and at an accelerated pace since the 1990s, the expectation of social and economic stability from cradle to grave, of working at a single job for one's whole life, in a traditional industry, has been supplanted by an "information economy," the actual contents or productiveness of which are not immediately apparent, and the stability of which is minimal. We have also seen the erosion of the autonomy and power of the secular state: free trade agreements, currency fluctuations, and increasing internationalism and the autonomy of corporate entities have tended to transfer especially economic power from the state to private corporations. Moreover, the internationalization of trade and economics has eroded social and cultural distinctions that could be taken utterly for granted even thirty years ago. I can no longer assume, for instance, that Canada's cultural identity is (at least partly) Christian; I do not need to go to the Middle East to see a mosque: they are all over Canada, as are various mixed-up traces of other cultures from all over the world. If I can experience "world culture" at home in Saskatchewan, then the concept of "a culture" has to be revised a great deal. My point is not that we Canadians and Americans are born racists who are disturbed by the presence of "other" cultures in our midst. Rather, I am suggesting that this mix, fostered by economic internationalism— globalism—is forcing upon us a redefinition of what culture *is*, and is in fact eroding the cultural distinctions—and identities based on them—that we have taken for granted in the past. For instance, we have tended in the past to associate culture with ethnic or national identity, and, as my examples suggest, this is no longer possible. Being a Muslim and a Canadian at the same time is not only possible, but common. Islamic religious (i.e., cultural) identity need not imply Middle Eastern national identity.

Whether we call it postmodernism or globalization, the relevance of this condition to historical Jesus reconstructions may not be immediately obvious, but strikes me as clear enough. What is at issue is offering some sort of response to the erosion or fragmentation of social and cultural identities, and the simultaneous homogenization of global culture that is implied by globalization or the postmodern condition.[23] What we see, then, in the differing presentations of the Jewish Jesus are different conceptualizations of what culture is, in the face of the need to respond, somehow, to its actual and inevitable reconfiguration in a "postmodern" world. As I have said elsewhere:

> Typically, this response is one of resistance. It sometimes manifests itself in a reaffirmation of the validity of that which is lost, its proponents behaving with idealist assumptions and imagining that the struggle to retain our souls is being fought at the level of ideas. With such an assumption, the response

involves the continual affirmation to the mind, with as much evidence as one can muster, that the concepts on which we base our worldview are still valid. The struggle for our souls, for our selves, for our very identities, therefore takes place at the level of asserting and intellectually defending those very comfortable and threatened conceptions—or means of conceptualizing—which are losing their resonance, in an effort to rebuild them, revivify them and thus once again live in a (conceptually) stable universe. (Arnal 1997b, 312)

This agenda, I suggest, is precisely what is behind some of the insistence on a reified Judaism in antiquity, and on a reified and anachronistic assertion of Jesus' "religion." What is being insisted upon here is precisely the *stability* of culture, and precisely the *distinctiveness* of cultural identity. If being a Jew can be easily and sharply defined, and if the application to a person of this classification can allow us easily to reconstruct their identity, then, by implication, my Canadian identity is likewise stable, clear, and distinctive. Here cultural distinctiveness and identity is being offered as a response and challenge in the face of conditions in which precisely these features of identity are becoming more and more questionable.

It is notable, in support of this claim, that Fredriksen's and Reinhartz's *Jesus, Judaism, and Christian Anti-Judaism*, a text ostensibly about ancient history and religion, opens with a preface that refers copiously to globalization, and sees in it a direct threat to distinctive religious identity:

Like a second Flood of biblical proportion, the global democratization of technology, finance, and information threatens to efface all that stands in its way…. [H]ow is it, amidst the homogenizing and totalizing power of economic globalization, that *particular* faith communities—like those of Judaism and Christianity—will be able to preserve, let alone deepen, their *specific religious* heritage? If our world's post-Cold War economy has proven itself no respecter of culture, neither will it be a respecter of religion. The implication … is clear: Jews and Christians are in the same boat. Both will struggle mightily to *preserve their own respective traditions* …. Both Christians and Jews face the common challenges of maintaining *particular* and *historically connected* faiths in the face of an impending deluge of economic globalization. (Newman 2002, ix–x; emphasis added)

Thus even among scholars who have no personal faith commitment to either Judaism or Christianity, a normative subtext may lurk behind their characterizations of the historical Jesus and of his "religion." Why, for instance, would a non-Christian scholar be interested in promoting the traditionalistic definition of religion, Judaism, and Christianity that I have suggested underlies some historical Jesus reconstructions? Because at issue is not simply the identity of Christianity, but the matter of identity itself.

Of course, this reaction to postmodernity is not the only one possible. Again, I have commented on this elsewhere:

The alternative, if one approaches the [postmodern] malaise from a materialist perspective, is to recognize that conceptions are products of the actual construction of the world of social humanity itself, and that the failure of certain conceptions to persist in a meaningful way is due less to intellectual stagnation than it is to a world whose human relations suggest different and changing patterns to the mind.... Since the subject or sense of personal/ human groundedness cannot be created ex *nihilo*, it must be constructed within and upon the material culture in which we now subsist, a task which requires not only working *with* the conceptual framework dictated by those circumstances but also changing those actual circumstances in such a way that we are left with a world better suited to modern human needs. Such a perspective lends itself to ignoring and even opposing conceptual archaisms such as "religion," and reifications thereof, including "Judaism." From this stance comes the passion and interest invested by advocates of the Cynic hypothesis and other opponents of the "Jesus the Jew" reconstruction, which derive from the assumption that these ideal conceptions are not only archaic and meaningless, but counterproductive. (Arnal 1997b, 312; emphasis original)

Thus again we see behind the alleged debate over a Jewish Jesus yet another subtext, in which "Jewish" is being offered as a cipher for the reification of cultural identity, religious or otherwise. Promotions of an identifiably and distinctively Jewish Jesus are resisting postmodern or globalizing homogenization and fragmentation precisely in their insistence on the coherence of "Jewish" identity. Reconstructions of a less visibly "Jewish" Jesus are offering their own response to postmodernism and globalization: not exactly an accommodation to its cultural tendencies, but a certain acceptance of the reality of current conditions, and a desire to work within those conditions for a better world, however that may be imagined.

When previously persuasive discourses no longer persuade and previously prevalent sentiments no longer prevail, society enters a situation of fluidity and crisis. In such moments, competing groups continue to deploy strategic discourses and may also make use of coercive force as they struggle, not just to seize or retain power, but to reshape the borders and hierarchic order of society itself. (Lincoln 1989, 174)

5 Conclusion

I have spent a great deal of time attempting to describe the undercurrents, the biases, the hidden agenda that I see lurking behind historical Jesus scholarship, both that with which I sympathize and that with which I emphatically disagree. The fact that such agenda can be claimed for *both* sides in the "debate," including scholars with whom I am in extensive agreement, should serve as an indication that I neither exempt myself from such subtextual interests nor regard their existence as an indication of the factual falsity of the scholarly conclusions with which they are associated. The one simply does not follow from the other. I have been accused in my own work on Q (particularly Arnal 2001a) of projecting my circumstances onto those of the Q people (whom I describe as, essentially, alienated low-level intellectuals, a characterization that *certainly* reflects my own self-conception) while criticizing others who do likewise. I can hardly deny the accusation, but at the same time the actual evidence I cite will support my reconstruction (or fail to, as the case may be) *regardless* of the congeniality of my conclusions. Indeed, I would claim—at least in those ephemeral moments of supreme self-confidence—that it is precisely the congeniality of these views that *allowed* me to see the historical *Sitz* behind Q accurately.

So likewise, I must stress that focusing on the subtext or cultural implications that may underlie the work of, say, Paula Fredriksen, is not in itself *any* indication that her views are wrong, and is not offered as such. Fredriksen, or Sanders, or Crossan, or Mack *could* indeed be so massively biased that their reconstructions of Jesus are nothing but projection; yet any one of those reconstructions could still be correct, and we owe it to these scholars to examine and assess the evidence they offer and the arguments they actually make, regardless of their personal agenda or the agenda behind the reception of their work. And it is equally true that scholarship which has no bias at all, should such an animal exist, could nonetheless produce a historical Jesus which is, factually speaking, one hundred percent wrong, or, alternatively, poorly argued. Our aim as scholars, therefore, must not and cannot be the impossible task of approaching our subject matters objectively. We cannot do so, and in my opinion as human beings we should not do so. Our job as scholars, rather, is to provide *reasons* for the claims we make, *reasons* for our rejections or approvals of the conclusions of our scholarly colleagues—and these reasons should, at least in theory, be comprehensible, assessable and "testable" by our scholarly peers. By "testable" I do not mean experimental testability as is expected in the natural sciences. I think this technique is probably impossible for the humanities. I simply mean that our arguments should be of a sort that any reasonable person should be able to assess them: they should not appeal to personal preferences, transcendent insights, or data that cannot be accessed by others.

I may vehemently dislike the *implications* of E. P. Sanders's Jesus and quite like the *implications* of Burton Mack's Jesus. My task as a scholar, however, is to keep my mind open to Sanders's arguments, and their potential strengths, as well as Mack's arguments, and their potential weaknesses. And should I conclude that I do, on scholarly grounds, think that Mack is more correct than Sanders, my reasons for this conclusion should be limited as much as possible to the cogency of their arguments. I must also stress that the issue here is my reaction to the *implications* of these reconstructions of Jesus, and not on my like or dislike of Jesus himself (as reconstructed). It has become fashionable in our field to assume that we will project the features we *like* onto the objects of our study: we will make Jesus or Paul or the Q people into replicas of ourselves. This strikes me as a presumptuous and simplistic notion of how bias works in our field. For some of us, there is simply no investment in Jesus, and no need to make him, in particular, "like us." Nor do I imagine that the Jesus of E. P. Sanders, for instance, actually reflects his own behavior (at least, I hope not). The point is rather in the way that the conceptualizations behind constructions of Jesus accord, or fail to accord, with our own worldviews, whether Jesus himself is presented as attractive or unattractive.

Naïve though it may be, I offer here a plea for a certain scholarly ethic, one that has been characterized by Bruce Lincoln as "mythology with footnotes" (Lincoln 1999, 209; cf. 207–16). As scholars, we are still human beings, and we in the humanities especially engage in the generation of human meaning, in the production of worldviews, in the *pensée sauvage* that organizes the universe around us. We are thus mythmakers ourselves even in our analysis of myth. In our reproductions of the historical Jesus, we are doing essentially the same thing that the gospel writers did, whether or not we are Christians or even attracted to the figure of Jesus: we are projecting our own beliefs onto a story (history) and so using narrative (of a sort) to create a myth. The responsibility that sets scholars apart from the more usual (especially religious) practitioners of myth-making is the care that we must take to *document* our claims, such that someday perhaps those claims may survive the inevitable desuetude of the myths they were designed to sustain. Perhaps one may add to this a plea for self-consciousness about the assumptions and agenda that influence one's work.[1]

Even this limited goal, however, may prove to be impossible in the long run. Yes, we study things because they matter to us, particularly in the humanities, and it would not occur to anyone to maintain an objective historiography by focusing on matters that no one cares about. There is a reason people keep writing books about Jesus' teaching, religion, and "ministry," but have failed to produce any scholarship on his dental hygiene, or on the length and cut of his fingernails and toenails.[2] Similarly, there is a reason people keep writing books on those aspects of *Jesus'* life that are deemed relevant, while failing to write books dealing with the same aspects of the life of, say, my grandmother, noble human being though she was. And this will remain true of all historical inquiry: we study things that matter to us, and do not bother to investigate material that may indeed constitute facts, raw data of some sort, but which concern people or issues that seem irrelevant or frivolous. We study things because they are important, directly or indirectly, implicitly or explicitly. This applies to all objects of historical inquiry, whether they are religious or not, and whether or not they carry the *degree* of cultural baggage that Jesus does. In the case of *historical* Jesus research, however, the ultimate motivations of the work and its methods may be so ill-founded and self-contradictory as to render the entire enterprise illegitimate from an academic perspective.

I base this suspicion on three considerations. The first is that the extent of Jesus' cultural prominence is so colossal that even purely historical inquiries will soon become so bogged down in current socio-cultural controversies as to become irrational, or, at the very least, lose sight of their (historical) subject. Indeed, the bulk of the foregoing study has revolved around this point. As I note above, it is not that we should study things that do not matter to us, or that we should aim for an impossible objectivity that brackets all forms of contemporary significance. But an inquiry that claims to be historical ought to actually be *about* its purported object, to at least some degree. Ironically, Jesus is *so* important that his historical reconstruction becomes *unimportant*, hopelessly overshadowed by its big brother, the Christ of faith.[3] That people who talk about Jesus are not *really* talking about Jesus at all was a point made brilliantly by Albert Schweitzer almost a hundred years ago (Schweitzer 1954 [1906]). It seems as valid an observation today as then.

My second—and related—consideration is that the nature of our sources for Jesus exacerbates the situation. While the object of our supposedly "historical" inquiry keeps transforming into a theological entity in front of our very eyes, the main sources on which we base our reconstructions present him as a theological entity in the first place.[4] Whether Jesus himself existed as a historical figure or not, the gospels that tell of him are unquestionably mythic texts. The Gospel of Mark, for example, is a narrative that includes a cast of characters comprising, *inter alia*, God, a son of God, angels, the devil, demons, holy spirits, evil spirits, and what seem to be the ghosts of Moses and Elijah. It is a story that features miraculous healings and exorcisms, as well as walking on water, feeding thousands of people with a handful of loaves and fishes (twice!), face-to-face conversations between people who lived centuries apart, spooky prognostications, trees withering at Jesus' simple command, a sun darkening in the middle of the day, and a temple curtain miraculously tearing itself in half. Investigations into the historical Jesus *require*, by contrast, that the gospels be used as historical sources, and in fact the main difference between "conservative" and "liberal" scholarship revolves around how much legendary accretion is stripped away in order to arrive at the "historical core," not whether there is any historical core to be found at all. In seeking to find the real, historical person behind these narratives, we are using these texts as sources for a figure that they themselves show no interest in at all. Just as the myths and legends about Herakles are simply not *about* a historical person, so also the gospels are not *about* the historical Jesus.

My third consideration is perhaps the most complex and controversial, but also the most important. I would claim that the *historical* Jesus is *historically* insignificant. As an entity, the historical Jesus is understood to be that figure who can be reconstructed with historical, rather than theological, methods, and who is important for history itself in some fashion. Those individuals (as opposed to conditions, processes, or events) who become objects of historical inquiry usually are judged appropriate for such investigation for quite definite and specific reasons. Most obvious are those people whose activity is regarded as having had an impact on the world around them, perhaps even as changing the course of history itself (e.g., Martin Luther King, Jr.). Other objects of historical inquiry, however, may be those people who, because of position or celebrity, are prominent in their own time, even if they accomplished or changed very little (e.g., Gerald Ford, Marilyn Monroe), or those people deemed to be typical and so studied as representative of the life and conditions of a given time and place. Historical Jesus scholars tend to treat Jesus as historically significant by the first of these criteria. He clearly is not regarded as a case study for the lives of ordinary people in Roman Palestine, and he simply cannot be described as a celebrity or publicly prominent figure in his own lifetime.

This means, then, that historical Jesus scholars assume that the relevance of Jesus as a historical person is as someone who accomplished something, did something, and thus changed the course of history. Since Jesus was no political or military figure, and never won a battle or occupied high office, the obvious accomplishment of his life was the initiation of a movement of religious reform that eventually became Christianity. Thus the ultimate goal of historical Jesus studies is to uncover the origins of Christianity itself, to reconstruct the Jesus who is assumed somehow to lie behind this movement as its root *cause*. The problem here is that the whole enterprise, thus conceived, rests on an exceptionally precarious set of assumptions. The notion that individuals *cause* or *found* religious movements is itself open to question on theoretical grounds. But at an even more basic level, the idea that the Christianity that came to dominate the Roman Empire and thence the world was the movement that Jesus himself caused or founded—as opposed to a movement revolving around an image of Jesus that was itself the product of mythmaking and legendary accretions—cannot be sustained, in part because of research into the historical Jesus himself. The discontinuity between the behavior and teaching of the historical Jesus as he is normally reconstructed and the beliefs and doctrines of what became the Christian religion is so vast as to make the assumption of any causal link between the two an instance of especially disgraceful special pleading.

And so perhaps the quest for the historical Jesus should be abandoned once again. Not because scholars cannot agree on their reconstructions; lack of agreement may only indicate that further—and more rigorous—work needs to be done. Not because the investigation has been biased; bias is unavoidable, here as elsewhere. Not even because reasonable conclusions are impossible in light of our defective sources, though this may indeed be the case. But because, ultimately, the *historical* Jesus does not matter, either for our understanding of the past, or our understanding of the present. The historically relevant and interesting causes of the development and growth of the Christian movement will be found, not in the person of Jesus, but in the collective machinations, agenda, and vicissitudes of the movement itself. And the Jesus who is important to our own day is not the Jesus of history, but the symbolic Jesus of contemporary discourse.

Endnotes

1. Introduction: Mad Mel and the Cultural Prominence of Jesus

1. The quotation is from Patty Bickerton, a youth minister at Glassport Assembly of God. It appears in "Easter Bunny whipped at church show; some families upset," in the Wednesday, April 7, 2004 edition of the Pittsburgh *Post-Gazette*, as an AP wire story. All subsequent quotations from the same story are also drawn from this brief article. Nearly identical versions appear at: http://www.msnbc.msn.com/id/4693430/, http://www.foxnews.com/story/0,2933,116560,00.html, and elsewhere.

2. Several commentators on Gibson's movie have pointed to various aspects of traditional Christian iconography as informing the visual "feel" of the movie, particularly the paintings of Caravaggio. But Medieval and early modern art aside, flagellation simply has not taken center stage in representations of the Passion in North America until 2004. One would especially not expect Protestant congregations to focus on views of the Passion taken from Medieval art. Gibson's movie, however, itself informed by a particularly traditionalist Roman Catholic piety, has been resoundingly popular with evangelical Protestant audiences, and so has served as a pipeline for older Roman Catholic imagery and tradition to enter American evangelical religiosity, essentially for the first time.

3. Take, for example, the notorious French anti-Semite, Jean-Marie Le Pen, who polled in second place for the French presidency in 2002. Le Pen has shifted from unpopular and rather pointless anti-Jewish rhetoric to a much more resonant anti-Arab (and concomitantly anti-immigrant) tone. One reporter comments as follows:

> According to some pollsters, it was the latest spate of anti-Semitic attacks in April that provided the final straw and convinced even more people to vote for Le Pen, who has long blamed local Arabs for many of France's woes. "It wasn't an election, it was a demonstration by the people of France against insecurity and violence," said Moise Cohen, the Moroccan-born president of the Paris Jewish religious board, the Consistoire. (Simon 2002)

Thus *Arab* attacks on Jews have generated *support* for a known anti-Semite precisely because his "anti-Semitism" extends to the Arabs responsible for these attacks.

2. Bad Karma: Anti-Semitism in New Testament Scholarship

1. Johnson (1986, 23) notes that: "An antisemitic bias in scholarly works of the time was certainly not due to ineptness or lack of knowledge; rather, we are faced with the perplexing fact that some of those whose knowledge of ancient Judaism was most thorough were willing to use scholarship for propagandistic ends."

2. Johnson (1986, 5) cites Georg Bertram, Johannes Leipoldt, Rudolph Meyer, Hans Pohlmann, Hugo Odeberg, and Friedrich Schenke, and offers an extended discussion of Gerhard Kittel.

3. See the detailed, insightful, and absolutely devastating discussion of the scholarly claims that Jesus and/or the earliest Christians were *unique* offered in Smith 1990.

4. This wonderful contrary-to-fact example of a Scandinavian Jesus is stolen outright, with gratitude, from Fredriksen 1999, 269.

5. Interestingly, Renan also comments on the "defects" of the "Semitic mind," and extends these supposed defects to Jesus himself (Renan 1935 [1863], 168–69):

> One of the principle defects of the Jewish race is its harshness in controversy and the abusive tone which it almost always infuses into it. There never were in the world such bitter quarrels as those of the Jews among themselves.... The lack of this faculty [of "nice discernment"] is one of the most constant features of the Semitic mind.... Jesus, who was exempt from almost all of the defects of his race, and whose leading quality was precisely an infinite delicacy, was led, in spite of himself, to make use of the general style in polemics.

6. On Freyne's comments see also Kloppenborg Verbin 2000b, 435. It should be noted that Freyne's own scholarly work has been especially concerned with stressing the religious *continuity* between Galilee and Judea. See especially Freyne 1980 and 1988.

7. See the devastating rejoinder to Wright in Kloppenborg Verbin 2000a, 86–94. Kloppenborg Verbin notes, among other things, that Wright has *invented* the opposition to a "Jewish" Q that he claims to find in Q scholarship; that many Q scholars deny that Q is Cynic; that none claim that Q is Gnostic; and that Wright has (along with too many others) wholly misunderstood the grounds for the stratification of Q.

8. The key figures behind the "Cynic hypothesis" are F. Gerald Downing (see Downing 1987, 1988); Burton L. Mack (see Mack 1997); Leif Vaage (see Vaage 1994); and David Seeley (see Seeley 1992). Extended criticisms of the "Cynic hypothesis" have been offered by, among many others, James M. Robinson (Robinson 1997); C. M. Tuckett (Tuckett 1989); Hans Dieter Betz (Betz 1994); and Paul Rhodes Eddy (Eddy 1996). For a discussion of these reactions see especially Kloppenborg Verbin 2000a, and my own efforts to characterize both the "Cynic hypothesis" and reactions to it (Arnal 2001a, 52–59).

9. I wish to thank Amy-Jill Levine for drawing this odd fact to my attention. Levine

suggests an entirely plausible explanation for this odd phenomenon that has nothing to do with any sort of anti-Semitic agenda on the part of third-world scholars. The libraries of deceased North American and Western European pastors are bequeathed to third-world institutions as a charitable act. These texts are of course outdated, and reflect attitudes and conclusions of the past, whether these be the mainstream conclusions of scholars such as Bultmann, Jeremias, and Käsemann, or the more offensive and pernicious views of a Chamberlain or a Grundmann. In the absence of more up-to-date works, some scholars fall back on the limited conclusions of works decades out of date.

10. For an excellent general discussion of white supremacist movements from a religious studies perspective, see Kaplan 1996.

3. A Manufactured Controversy: Why the "Jewish Jesus" is a Red Herring

1. John Kloppenborg has also been associated with this scholarly trajectory, although his work has not typically focused on the historical Jesus.

2. It is striking that Reed recognizes the affinity between the questions he poses about Galilean identity and the anti-Semitic agenda of earlier scholars, but of course is careful to note that he is working with completely different assumptions and agenda:

> Discovering the identity of the Galileans in the first century underlies any study of the historical Jesus and reconstruction of Christian origins. While an earlier generation debated the issue under the shadow of Nazi racial theories and scurrilous attempts at an Aryan Jesus, the recent discussion's impetus is the recognition of diversity in early Judaism and the role of regionalism as a factor in historical reconstruction. The present study is indebted to both of these recognitions and is much less concerned with the Galileans' racial identity in genetic or biological terms, but focuses rather on the Galileans' ethnic identity in terms of their socialized patterns of behavior, including religious aspects embedded in this behavior. (Reed 2000, 23)

3. In particular, Mack draws his conclusions from the logic and literary forms of (1) the earliest stratum of Q, more or less as identified by John Kloppenborg (Kloppenborg 1987); and (2) the pre-Markan pronouncement stories. See Mack 1988, 57–62; 2001a, 42–51.

4. And this in spite of the fact that Josephus, himself a first-century Jew, feels perfectly free to characterize Jewish sectarian movements as "philosophies" (*philosopheitai, philosophiai*; see *Antiquities* 18.14–25; *War* 2.117–66) and at times makes explicit comparisons and even identifications between Jewish beliefs and those of Greeks, including philosophers. He identifies Judas the Galilean, for instance, as a Sophist (*sophistēs*; *War* 2.118); the afterlife beliefs of the Essenes are said to be shared with the Greeks (*War* 2.155–56); and he explicitly compares the Pharisees to the Stoics (*Life* 12). My point is not that there is anything at all unusual about

these comparisons, but precisely the opposite: comparison or even identification of Judaism with the beliefs and practices of other Greco-Roman cultures was allowable and even natural for first-century Jews themselves.

5. See the discussions in Arnal 2001a, 52–59; Kloppenborg Verbin 2000a; 2000b, 420–32; Seeley 1992; Vaage 1994; cf. Mack 2001a, 54–58.

6. See especially his treatment in the final chapter of *Myth of Innocence* (Mack 1988), and in his three articles in Part 3 ("Tracing the Logic and Legacy," 127–93) of *The Christian Myth: Origins, Logic, and Legacy* (Mack 2001b).

7. Meier's comments are more temperate (and accurate) in Meier 1999, 484–85.

8. Meier's comments as quoted above appear in a work with a publication date of 2001. Crossan's *Who Killed Jesus?* was published in 1995; Mack's *Myth of Innocence* in 1988.

9. I.e., as above, Sanders 2002; Wright 1992; Pearson 1996. For a compelling discussion of this and other reactions to the Jesus Seminar, see especially Miller 1999.

10. I am, alas, referring primarily to my own regrettably harsh review of Paula Fredriksen's *Jesus of Nazareth, King of the Jews* (Fredriksen 1999), in which I accuse her of "duplicity" (among other things) in her treatment of the historical Jesus (Arnal 2000b). At the same time, I also think this particular book descends almost to the level of ridicule in its treatment of opposing positions (e.g., especially Fredriksen 1999, 269). Note also that Robert Miller, in responding to some critics of the Jesus Seminar, feels the need to make statements such as this: "This chapter is slightly revised from its original publication ... Several of my remarks there are mean-spirited and needlessly divert attention from the real issues. I apologize to Professor Witherington and ask anyone who might quote from or refer to my critique of *The Jesus Quest* to use the more civil version in this chapter" (Miller 1999, 109).

11. I note, by the way, that this is a formulation that Burton Mack in particular resists. Mack sees the genesis of a distinctive Christianity as having little or nothing to do with the historical Jesus, and everything to do with the social processes impinging on subsequent "followers" of Jesus. Such a view allows for a Jesus who is perfectly ordinary. While I am sympathetic to Mack's general point here, I would insist that *if* we are to recover a *historical* Jesus—i.e., a figure who is identifiable and who in some way can be understood as a causal factor in later Christian beliefs—then this figure must be distinctive in some fashion, given that he is reconstructed as in some way a cause of a distinctive movement. I am not sure, however, that such a figure *can* be reconstructed at all. See my concluding comments in Chapter 5.

12. See also the comment of Schüssler Fiorenza 2000, 40–41:

> Yet, whereas the Second Quest stressed the difference of the "feminist" Jesus over and against Judaism, the Third Quest argues for his integration into his patriarchal Jewish society and religion. Jesus was a devout Jewish man who did not question the dominant structures of his society but fully subscribed to them. If the dissimilarity criterion is replaced with the criterion of plausibility within a kyriarchal frame of reference, one cannot but reconstruct Jesus' Jewishness in terms of the dominant patriarchal ethos of the first century. At this point the entrapping character of this new criterion in Historical-Jesus research becomes obvious.

13. This observation requires special stress because it also applies to another supposed index of "common" Judaism in antiquity: purity. Even if it is the case that an interest in purity considerations were typical of nearly all Jews in antiquity, this interest hardly marked them off from anyone else in the Mediterranean. It is a feature not of Judaism, but of ancient anthropology, religion, and social life in general. So also, ironically enough, Sanders 2002, 36; emphasis original: *"The rituals of ancient people who lived around the Mediterranean Sea were all approximately the same."*

14. Philip Harland (2004) offers an analysis of Jewish grave inscriptions in Hierapolis that is remarkably complementary of Smith's conclusions. Focusing on one particular family gravesite, Harland concludes that:

> While many Jewish families did assert their identity (in relation to non-Jews) by using the designation "Jew/Judean" (*Ioudaioi*), the Glykon inscription stands out among the epitaphs of Hierapolis, and even Asia Minor or the empire, in its special concern to carry on Jewish *observances* even after death, thereby continuing to express this identity within Hierapolis indefinitely. At the same time, Glykon felt himself to be a Roman, both in proudly indicating his status as Roman citizen and by choosing to include the Roman New Year's festival as a time when the family would be remembered…. Alongside this Jewish-Roman identity, the family clearly experienced a sense of belonging within the community of Hierapolis specifically in many respects. (Harland 2004, 44; emphasis original)

15. It seems to me that Fredriksen 1999, 284–85, comes perilously close to such an assertion. Here she notes the features that distinguish first-century "Jewish" society (I assume she is referring specifically to Judean-Palestinian Jewish society) from both the broader Roman cultural overlay and from the social features of our own time. This is all well and good (if possibly mistaken in certain specifics), but the overall effect is to suggest that comparison should not be undertaken at all, and especially that overarching analytic structures, e.g., those based on economics, should not be applied to Jewish antiquity. Apparently Jewish "religion" (itself an anachronism) vitiated entirely the social effects of economic disparities!

16. This is true also of charges of racism in general. Americans in particular live in a violently racist society, but deflect attention from this social fact by expending their energy focusing on trivial *cultural* slights. Pseudo-issues such as whether American blacks should be called "African-American" direct our attention away from important social phenomena, such as the grossly disproportionate number of blacks in American prisons. The charge of racism should be reserved for real racism: there is more than enough to go around without inventing it.

4. The Jewish Jesus and Contemporary Identity

1.   Note the famous fact that the Jesus Seminar, applying techniques similar to those of the post-Bultmannian "second quest," arrived at a figure of only 18 percent of the total sayings attributed to Jesus in ancient texts being authentic. For discussion, see Miller 1999, 76, 113.

2.   Sanders worked at Oxford University from 1984–1990. His degree, however, is from Union Seminary, New York, and he is currently at Duke University. He also worked in Canada for some time, at McMaster University in Hamilton, Ontario.

3.   Regarding sayings material, only fifteen sayings (and versions thereof) are colored red by the Jesus Seminar. See Funk, Hoover, and the Jesus Seminar 1993, 549. As for Sanders's "indisputable facts," several, including for instance the call of the twelve, are rejected decisively as unhistorical by the Jesus Seminar. See the table in Funk and the Jesus Seminar 1998, 558–64.

4.   Note, however, that some of the scholars who have been criticized for producing a "non-Jewish" Jesus have also rejected this criterion. See Mack's comments—in this instance rather harsh—on the Jesus Seminar (Mack 2001b, 35):

> … the Jesus Seminar used criteria such as the principles of "dissimilarity" and "most difficult reading" on the assumption that sayings coming from Jesus must have been unique, novel, without cultural precedence, and therefore catching, surprising, important, and capable of changing the way people thought (and think!).

I myself think that the criterion is problematic because of the assumption that later "Christians" were not themselves distinctive in their own right. It is also enormously difficult to discern what *was* distinctive: the application of this criterion assumes, counterfactually, that we know everything there is to know about ancient culture.

5.   The slayers in this case are both men and women; but the slain are quite exclusively men: hence my use of exclusive language here. Were we to have any foremothers in this wildly androcentric field of ours, I would recommend slaying them too. But that, alas, will be a task for the *next* generation of scholars.

6.   This, it seems to me, is much of the gist of Fredriksen and Reinhartz, *Jesus, Judaism, and Christian Anti-Judaism* (2002). The book does offer some very critical essays that expose the anti-Jewish roots of Christianity, but the overall thrust of the text appears to me as an effort to deny the anti-Jewish origins of the Christian religion, and so to explain (later) Christian anti-Judaism as an aberration or deviation.

7.   Please note that I am not suggesting for instant that this is so. All of these texts or assertions are clearly polemical fabrications.

8.   The relevance, however, of *canon* is another matter. Note in addition that I am assuming throughout this book that historical reconstruction can and does function as cryptic promotion of ideology. But my point here is that history, or better, historiography, *as discourse*, does speak to the present. This need not require, however, that the actual events of the past, especially the distant past, need speak this way. The past does not speak at all; historians speak for it.

9.   Efforts that at times strike me as boiling down to little more than the claim that "some of my best friends (and Gods) are Jews."

10. One could quibble about what this statement means, but given the way Luke periodizes history, my sense is that Luke understands the "fulfillment" of the "times of the Gentiles" as the last stage before the ushering in of the apocalypse.

11. I must register my discomfort, however, with Fredriksen's casual implication that anti-Zionism is more or less equivalent to anti-Judaism or anti-Semitism, or that the former is always motivated by the latter. Indeed, she actually describes anti-Zionism as an "avatar" of anti-Judaism. While I am sure she does not intend this, one must nevertheless be extraordinarily careful not to extend the charge of anti-Semitism to any criticisms of the behavior of people who just happen to be Jews. Indeed, the sloppy accusation of anti-Semitism to anyone critical of Zionism on political or moral grounds, or to anyone critical of any of the actions of the state of Israel, or to anyone at all concerned about the conditions and treatment of Palestinians is appallingly offensive. It not only misuses a grave moral accusation to short-circuit moral inquiry itself, but it also misconstrues and cheapens the charge of anti-Semitism, in exactly the same way—although with much greater consequence, on a much more important issue—as when the charge is used as a *tour de force* in biblical arguments, as discussed above.

Both among Zionists themselves, and among modern anti-Semitic fringe groups, there seems to be a strange association offered between Zionism and the Holocaust. For the former, the Holocaust itself is rationale enough for the existence of the state of Israel, but, in addition, this correlation may be used to imply that any critique of Israel is anti-Semitic (a position that does not make sense). Thus one sometimes encounters "rebuttals" of criticisms of Israeli actions, particularly toward Palestinians, with invocations of the Holocaust, a powerful rhetorical move but one that has nothing to do with the issue at hand. The linkage, oddly enough, also seems to be endorsed by the most hateful of modern anti-Semitic "white power" groups. There the Holocaust is somehow relativized or even justified by appeal to Israeli treatment of Palestinians, as if the two issues had any logical connection at all. This strange and illogical linkage serves to cloud any reasonable or intelligent discussion of any of the issues involved, and so is to be profoundly regretted. For an excellent, if at times harsh, discussion of contemporary accusations of anti-Semitism in political discourse, see Cockburn and St. Clair 2003.

12. Note of course all the qualifications I have already offered about this alleged characterization of Jesus. The point of Vaage's or Mack's arguments is not that Jesus was a Cynic but that Jesus may be compared to a Cynic. Nonetheless I am here presenting the straw man that has been so often criticized, since it is the critique itself I am focusing on now, and not the original hypothesis.

13. See, however, the extended and convincing argument for *Thomas*'s independence from the synoptics offered in Patterson 1993. So far, I have yet to find a compelling refutation of Patterson's claims; indeed, my own work on *Thomas* has convinced me that Patterson's argument is actually understated. Meier's arguments regarding *Thomas* in volume one of *A Marginal Jew* cannot even be taken seriously. A recent claim has been made, however, that *Thomas* is dependent on the Diatessaron and was originally composed in Syriac: so Perrin 2002.

14. I want to stress that *very* few scholars use *Thomas* as the primary source for their reconstructions of Jesus. Crossan, the Jesus Seminar, and others typically use *Thomas* as one source, alongside Q, Mark, and even singly-attested material from Matthew and Luke. The complaint is not, in most cases, that *Thomas* has been used exclusively or predominantly, but that it has been used at all. This is especially clear in Pearson 1996, 15–16, where he complains that the Jesus Seminar attempted to use *Thomas*, but then goes on to acknowledge that *Thomas* had no influence at all on the resulting portrait of Jesus.

15. I am focusing on Mark because it serves as the source for the bulk of narrative material in Matthew and Luke. Thus concentration on reconstructing especially the activity of Jesus from the three synoptic gospels boils down to information ultimately derived from Mark. I have noted elsewhere (Arnal 1997a) that Sanders's list of "indisputable facts" about Jesus is little more than a plot summary of the Gospel of Mark.

16. I chose this example because it is *not* susceptible to the claim that what is at issue is halakhic debate over the fine points of Sabbath observance. It is clear from Jesus' response in Mark that he is denying the applicability of Sabbath regulations (at least their applicability to himself), not disputing what they are.

17. While Levine (2002, 82–83) quite correctly notes that Mark is much more overtly hostile to particular Jewish groups than to Jews in general, the one shades over into the other in the account of Pilate's offer to free Jesus in Mark 15:6–15. Mark does stress that the crowds called for Jesus' execution because "the chief priests stirred up the crowd" (15:11), but it is still precisely that generalized "crowd" that cries out, "crucify him," when Pilate asks about what should be done with Jesus (Mark 15:13–14). Matthew's gloss on this passage, "and all the people answered, 'his blood be on us and on our children'" (Matt 27:25), merely makes explicit what Mark has already implied.

I should note that my own reading of Mark's attitudes toward "Jewish" responsibility for Jesus' death are rather more complex than I have let on here, and certainly more debatable. I follow Burton Mack's reconstruction of Mark's agenda as he expresses it in *A Myth of Innocence* (1988), in which Mark lays the blame for Jesus' death directly upon the Jewish people, and views the destruction of the temple (for Mack—and I agree—Mark post-dates 70 CE) both as an act of divine vengeance and as a prelude to a coming apocalyptic consummation. Such a reading is based on fairly detailed examination of Mark's passion narrative, and this material is obviously subject to different interpretations. I myself cannot help but see the daytime darkness and the tearing of the temple curtain at Jesus' death (Mark 15:33, 38) as allusions to the apocalyptic events "predicted" in Mark 13 and to the events of the Jewish War. Thus it seems to me that the parable of the tenants in Mark serves as an allegory for the whole narrative logic of Mark: the tenants of the vineyard (i.e., Israel) kill the son and so reap destruction for themselves (though, I note, Levine [2002, 86] disagrees with such a reading). This very particular view of Mark, however, need not be accepted for my basic point here to stand, which is simply that Mark possesses a variety of "non-Jewish" and "anti-Jewish" features.

18. Saying #65 lacks entirely the allegorical dimensions that make the version in

Mark 12:1–9 so polemical. John Kloppenborg Verbin, as well, has recently shown that the version in *Thomas* is not only more original than that in Mark, but that the parable's allusion to Isa 5:1–7, in *Mark's* version, is drawn from the LXX and assumes Egyptian viticultural techniques, while that of *Thomas* is more realistic and reflects Palestinian viticulture. See Kloppenborg Verbin 2000c.

19. Even Matthew's version (Matt 22:1–14), for all of its suspicion of the negative consequences of a Gentile mission (see 22:10–14), understands the parable in this fashion, and, moreover, emphasizes the motif that a gentile mission is akin to punishment—along with the destruction of Jerusalem! (22:7)—for Jewish misdeeds, both by associating the call to Gentiles with the violence of the original proposed guests (as opposed to Luke's version [Luke 14:16–24], where they simply reject the invitation rather than killing those who offer it); and in his positioning of it immediately after his version of the parable of the tenants (Matt 21:33–46), where the same motifs are developed.

20. That is, the use of a "signature" element of one particular style to allude to that style in a building whose style is completely different. An example would be the use of high Corinthian columns on the façade of a small private dwelling.

21. This is part of the problem with N. T. Wright's criticism of Crossan (Wright 1993). He seems to assume that "postmodernism" is merely a philosophical theory, to which one might offer reasonable alternatives. To put it differently, Crossan's alleged "postmodernism" should be assessed as a *symptom*, not as the assertion of a philosophical model.

22. Predictably, "postmodernism" as a positive term and as an academic movement has proved to be something of an ephemeral trend.

23. The irony or contradiction here is only superficial. That national or traditional cultural identities are being eroded does not necessarily bring with it an end to totalizing conceptions of human behavior. Quite the reverse: the failure of national and cultural identities to retain their salience by retaining their boundaries opens the door to a totalizing global culture based solely on consumerism. If both the Buddha and Mohammed have been set aside, the vacuum may be filled in both instances with McDonalds and Disney World.

5. Conclusion

1. So also Martin 2001, 59:

> While I certainly would not want to contend that the exegetical or theological debates among scholars were unimportant or merely secondary to other, more "real" issues, it is nonetheless obvious that treatments of the Hellenism and Judaism of Paul and early Christianity are absolutely implicated in other contemporary debates. I do not mean to imply that we should attempt to extricate ourselves from our surroundings or work to be "objective" or "disinterested" in our research, as if we could keep our own concerns from affecting our historical work. I do suggest, though, that we might be better off, or at least less predictable and therefore more

interesting, if we recognize our own interests and contingencies and acknowledge how they relate to our readings.

2. It would be folly for me to claim that these subjects will never be broached, since what has been viewed as utterly trivial to date may become significant at some future time, for unpredictable reasons. Aspects of Jesus' personal appearance and dress, for instance, *have* been discussed, and continue to be discussed, or at least are embedded as tropes in the popular imagination about Jesus. The length of Jesus' hair, for instance, has been the subject of historical inquiry as well as pious imagination. Likewise, just about any representation of Jesus without facial hair (e.g., the dust jacket on Meier 1991, but cf. the cover of Meier 2001) or wearing the wrong footwear, e.g., boots, will likely elicit a negative reaction, even if those who react thus are not quite sure what is bothering them—simply because we think of Jesus as necessarily being bearded and wearing sandals. There may be no particularly weighty reason for this; it is just how we imagine him.

3. Even those scholars who are not themselves Christians, and so have no Christ of faith of their own to protect, are nonetheless cognizant of and perforce engaged with the monumental significance of this theological entity for the majority of the people surrounding them.

4. I am deliberately avoiding here the question of non-Christian sources for Jesus, such as Tacitus or Josephus, and focusing exclusively on the gospels. While the references to Jesus in the works of such non-Christian historians are occasionally used to support reconstructions of Jesus as a historical person, they actually provide next to no information at all. If people restricted themselves to what Josephus, for instance, says about Jesus, there would not be enough information for a short article, never mind a book. I am also convinced that the only possible sources for these "historical" descriptions of Jesus must have been Christian sources, oral or written. If so, then even these non-Christian descriptions of Jesus ultimately reflect only Christian perceptions of him.

Bibliography

Arnal, William E. 1995. "The Rhetoric of Marginality: Apocalypticism, Gnosticism, and Sayings Gospels." *Harvard Theological Review* 88/4: 471–94.

—1997a. "Major Episodes in the Biography of Jesus: Methodological Observations on the Historicity of the Narrative Tradition." *Toronto Journal of Theology* 13/2: 201–26.

—1997b. "Making and Re-Making the Jesus-Sign: Contemporary Markings on the Body of Christ." In William E. Arnal and Michel Desjardins, eds., *Whose Historical Jesus?*, 308–19. Waterloo, Ontario: Wilfrid Laurier University Press.

—2000a. "Definition (of Religion)." In Willi Braun and Russell T. McCutcheon, eds., *Guide to the Study of Religion*, 21–34. London and New York: Cassell.

—2000b. Review of Paula Fredriksen, *Jesus of Nazareth, King of the Jews. Jewish Quarterly Review* 110/3-4: 439–42.

—2001a. *Jesus and the Village Scribes: Galilean Conflicts and the Setting of Q.* Minneapolis: Fortress.

—2001b. "The Segregation of Social Desire: 'Religion' and Disney World." *Journal of the American Academy of Religion* 69/1: 1–19.

Asad, Talal. 1993. "The Construction of Religion as an Anthropological Category." In *Genealogies of Religion: Discipline and Reasons of Power in Christianity and Islam*, 27–54. Baltimore: Johns Hopkins University Press.

Associated Press. 2004. "Easter Bunny whipped at church show; some families upset." In the Pittsburgh *Post-Gazette*, April 7, 2004.

Baird, William. 1992. *History of New Testament Research, I: From Deism to Tübingen.* Minneapolis: Fortress.

Barrett, C. K. 1968. *Jesus and the Gospel Tradition.* Philadelphia: Fortress.

Betz, Hans Dieter. 1994. "Jesus and the Cynics: Survey and Analysis of a Hypothesis." *Journal of Religion* 74: 453–75.

Bultmann, Rudolf. 1951. *Theology of the New Testament*, 2 vols. Trans. Kendrick Grobel. New York: Charles Scribner's Sons.

Canadian Broadcasting Corporation (CBC) News Online Staff. 2004a. "Prime Minister condemns attack on Montreal Jewish School." Canadian Broadcasting Corporation, April 5, 2004, http://www.cbc.ca/stories/2004/04/05/canada/mtlschool040405.

—2004b. "5 arrested in Montreal Jewish school bombing." Canadian Broadcasting Corporation, May 14, 2004, http://www.cbc.ca/stories/2004/05/14/canada/firebomb_040514.

Chamberlain, Houston Stewart. 1977 [1899]. *Foundations of the Nineteenth Century*, 2 vols. Trans. John Lees. New York: Howard Fertig.

Chilton, Bruce D. 1984. *A Galilean Rabbi and His Bible: Jesus' Use of the Interpreted Scripture of His Time.* Wilmington, DE: Michael Glazier.

Cockburn, Alexander, and Jeffrey St. Clair, eds. 2003. *The Politics of Anti-Semitism.* Edinburgh, London, Oakland: AK Press.

Crossan, John Dominic. 1991. *The Historical Jesus: The Life of a Mediterranean Jewish Peasant*. New York: HarperCollins.

—1994. *Jesus: A Revolutionary Biography*. San Francisco: HarperSanFrancisco.

—1995. *Who Killed Jesus? Exposing the Roots of Anti-Semitism in the Gospel Story of the Death of Jesus*. San Francisco: HarperSanFrancisco.

Daly, Mary, in cohoots with Jane Caputi. 1987. *Websters' First New Intergalactic Wickedary of the English Language*. Boston: Beacon.

Davies, Alan T. 1975. "The Aryan Christ: A Motif in Christian Anti-Semitism." *Journal of Ecumenical Studies* 12/4: 569–79.

Davis, Walter A. 2004. "The Bite of the Whip: Passion of the Christ in Abu Ghraib." *Counterpunch*, June 19/20, 2004, http://www.counterpunch.org/davis06192004.html.

De Conick, April D. 2002. "The Original Gospel of Thomas." *Vigiliae Christianae* 56/2: 167–99.

Downing, F. Gerald. 1987. *Jesus and the Threat of Freedom*. London: SCM.

—1988. *Christ and the Cynics: Jesus and Other Radical Preachers in First-Century Tradition*. Sheffield: JSOT Press.

Eddy, Paul Rhodes. 1996. "Jesus as Diogenes? Reflections on the Cynic Jesus." *Journal of Biblical Literature* 115: 449–69.

Ericksen, Robert P. 1999. "Assessing the Heritage: German Protestant Theologians, Nazis, and the 'Jewish Question.'" In Robert P. Ericksen and Susannah Heschel, eds., *Betrayal: German Churches and the Holocaust*, 22–39. Minneapolis: Fortress.

Fredriksen, Paula. 1999. *Jesus of Nazareth, King of the Jews: A Jewish Life and the Emergence of Christianity*. New York: Knopf.

—2002. "The Birth of Christianity and the Origins of Christian Anti-Judaism." In Paula Fredriksen and Adele Reinhartz, eds., *Jesus, Judaism, and Christian Anti-Judaism: Reading the New Testament after the Holocaust*, 8–30. Louisville, KY and London: Westminster John Knox.

—2003. "Mad Mel: The Gospel According to Gibson." In *New Republic*, July 28: 25–28.

Fredriksen, Paula, and Adele Reinhartz, eds. 2002. *Jesus, Judaism, and Christian Anti-Judaism: Reading the New Testament after the Holocaust*. Louisville, KY and London: Westminster John Knox.

Freyne, Seán. 1980. *Galilee from Alexander the Great to Hardian, 323 B.C.E to 135 C.E.: A Study of Second Temple Judaism*. Wilmington, DE: Michael Glazier.

—1988. *Galilee, Jesus, and the Gospels: Literary Approaches and Historical Investigations*. Philadelphia: Fortress.

—1997. "Galilean Questions to Crossan's Mediterranean Jesus." In William E. Arnal and Michel Desjardins, eds., *Whose Historical Jesus?*, 63–91. Waterloo, Ontario: Wilfrid Laurier University Press.

Funk, Robert W., Ray Hoover, and the Jesus Seminar. 1993. *The Five Gospels: What did Jesus Really Say?* New York: Macmillan.

Funk, Robert W., and the Jesus Seminar. 1998. *The Acts of Jesus: What did Jesus Really Do?* San Francisco: HarperSanFrancisco.

Grundmann, Walter. 1940. *Jesus der Galiläer und das Judentum*. Leipzig: Georg Wigand.

Hanson, K. C., and Douglas E. Oakman. 1998. *Palestine in the Time of Jesus: Social Structures and Social Conflicts.* Minneapolis: Fortress.

Harland, Philip A. 2004. "Acculturation and Identity in the Diaspora: A Jewish Family and 'Pagan' Guilds in Hierapolis." Unpublished paper read at the annual meeting of the Canadian Society of Biblical Studies, Winnipeg, June 1, 2004.

Harvey, David. 1989. *The Condition of Postmodernity: An Enquiry into the Origins of Cultural Change.* Oxford: Blackwell.

Hays, Richard. 1994. "The Corrected Jesus." *First Things* (May 1994): 43–48.

Hengel, Martin. 1989. *The "Hellenization" of Judaea in the First Century after Christ.* London: SCM Press.

Heschel, Susannah. 1994. "Nazifying Christian Theology: Walter Grundmann and the Institute for the Study and Eradication of Jewish Influence on German Church Life." *Church History* 63/4 (December 1994): 587–605.

Horsley, Richard A. 1995. *Galilee: History, Politics, People.* Valley Forge, PA: Trinity Press International.

—1996. *Archaeology, History, and Society in Galilee: The Social Context of Jesus and the Rabbis.* Harrisburg, PA: Trinity Press International.

Hurtado, Larry W. 1997. "A Taxonomy of Recent Historical-Jesus Work." In William E. Arnal and Michel Desjardins, eds., *Whose Historical Jesus?*, 272–95. Waterloo, Ontario: Wilfrid Laurier University Press.

Jameson, Frederic. 1991. *Postmodernism; Or, The Cultural Logic of Late Capitalism.* Durham, NC: Duke University Press.

Jeremias, Joachim. 1965. *The Central Message of the New Testament.* New York: Charles Scribner's Sons.

Johnson, Luke Timothy. 1996. *The Real Jesus: The Misguided Quest for the Historical Jesus and the Truth of the Traditional Gospels.* San Francisco: HarperSanFrancisco.

Johnson, Marshall D. 1986. "Power Politics and New Testament Scholarship in the National Socialist Period." *Journal of Ecumenical Studies* 23/1: 1–24.

Kaplan, Jeffrey. 1996. *Radical Religion in America: Millenarian Movements from the Far Right to the Children of Noah.* Syracuse, NY: Syracuse University Press.

Käsemann, Ernst. 1964. "The Problem of the Historical Jesus." In *Essays on New Testament Themes*, 15–47. Philadelphia: Fortress.

Khan, Shahnaz. 2002. *Aversion and Desire: Negotiating Muslim Female Identity in the Diaspora.* Toronto: Women's Press.

Kittel, Gerhard, ed., and Geoffrey W. Bromiley, trans. and ed. 1964–76. *Theological Dictionary of the New Testament.* Grand Rapids, MI: Eerdmans.

Kloppenborg, John S. 1987. *The Formation of Q: Trajectories in Ancient Wisdom Collections.* Philadelphia: Fortress.

Kloppenborg Verbin, John. 2000a. "A Dog among the Pigeons: The 'Cynic Hypothesis' as a Theological Problem." In Jon Ma. Asgeirsson, Kristin de Troyer, and Marvin W. Meyer, eds., *From Quest to Q: Festschrift James M. Robinson*, 73–117. Leuven: Leuven University Press.

—2000b. *Excavating Q: The History and Setting of the Sayings Gospel.* Minneapolis: Fortress.

—2000c. "Isaiah 5:1-7, The Parable of the Tenants and Vineyard Leases on Papyrus."

In Stephen G. Wilson and Michel Desjardins, eds., *Text and Artifact in the Religions of Mediterranean Antiquity: Essays in Honour of Peter Richardson*, 111–34. Waterloo, Ontario: Wilfrid Laurier University Press.

Levine, Amy-Jill. 2002. "Matthew, Mark, and Luke: Good News or Bad?" In Paula Fredriksen and Adele Reinhartz, eds., *Jesus, Judaism, and Christian Anti-Judaism: Reading the New Testament after the Holocaust*, 77–98. Louisville, KY and London: Westminster John Knox.

Lincoln, Bruce. 1989. *Discourse and the Construction of Society: Comparative Studies of Myth, Ritual, and Classification*. New York and Oxford: Oxford University Press.

—1999. *Theorizing Myth: Narrative, Ideology, and Scholarship*. Chicago: University of Chicago Press.

Mack, Burton L. 1988. *A Myth of Innocence: Mark and Christian Origins*. Philadelphia: Fortress.

—1993. *The Lost Gospel: The Book of Q and Christian Origins*. San Francisco: HarperSanFrancisco.

—1997. "Q and a Cynic-Like Jesus." In William E. Arnal and Michel Desjardins, eds., *Whose Historical Jesus?*, 25–36. Waterloo, Ontario: Wilfrid Laurier University Press.

—2001a. "The Case for a Cynic-Like Jesus." In *idem, The Christian Myth: Origins, Logic, and Legacy*, 41–58. New York: Continuum.

—2001b. *The Christian Myth: Origins, Logic, and Legacy*. New York: Continuum.

Martin, Dale. 2001. "Paul and the Judaism / Hellenism Dichotomy: Toward a Social History of the Question." In Troels Engberg-Pedersen, ed., *Paul Beyond the Judaism / Hellenism Divide*, 29–61. Louisville, KY: Westminster John Knox.

Martin, Luther H. 1987. *Hellenistic Religions: An Introduction*. New York: Oxford University Press.

Meacham, Jon. 2004. "Who Killed Jesus?" *Newsweek*, February 16, 2004: 44–53.

Meier, John P. 1991. *A Marginal Jew: Rethinking the Historical Jesus*. Vol. I. New York: Doubleday.

—1999. "The Present State of the 'Third Quest' for the Historical Jesus: Loss and Gain." *Biblica* 80: 459–86.

—2001. *A Marginal Jew: Rethinking the Historical Jesus*, III: *Companions and Competitors*. New York: Doubleday.

Miller, Robert J. 1999. *The Jesus Seminar and its Critics*. Santa Rosa, CA: Polebridge Press.

Miller, Robert J., ed. 2001. *The Apocalyptic Jesus: A Debate*. Santa Rosa, CA: Polebridge Press.

Moore, Stephen D. 1989. *Literary Criticism and the Gospels: The Theoretical Challenge*. New Haven: Yale University Press.

Neill, S., and T. Wright. 1988. *The Interpretation of the New Testament 1861–1986*. Oxford: Oxford University Press.

Neumann, Michael. 2004. "A Happy Compromise: Hate Crime Reporting in the Toronto *Globe and Mail*." In *Counterpunch*, April 14, 2004, http://www. counterpunch.org/neumann04152004.html.

Newman, Carey C. 2002. "Foreword." In Paula Fredriksen and Adele Reinhartz, eds., *Jesus, Judaism, and Christian Anti-Judaism: Reading the New Testament after the Holocaust*, ix–xi. Louisville, KY and London: Westminster John Knox.

Patterson, Stephen J. 1993. *The Gospel of Thomas and Jesus*. Sonoma, CA: Pole-
    bridge Press.
Pearson, Birger A. 1996. "The Gospel According to the Jesus Seminar." *Occasional
    Papers of the Institute for Antiquity and Christianity* 35. The Claremont Graduate
    School, April 1996.
Perrin, Nicholas. 2002. *Thomas and Tatian: The Relationship Between the Gospel of
    Thomas and the Diatessaron*. Leiden: Brill.
Perrin, Norman. 1967. *Rediscovering the Teaching of Jesus*. New York: Harper & Row.
Perrin, Norman, and Dennis C. Duling. 1982. *The New Testament: An Introduction*,
    2nd ed. San Diego: Harcourt Brace Jovanovich.
Reed, Jonathan L. 2000. *Archaeology and the Galilean Jesus: A Re-examination of the
    Evidence*. Harrisburg, PA: Trinity Press International.
Renan, Ernest. 1935 [1863]. *The Life of Jesus*. The Thinker's Library, 53. London:
    Watts & Co.
Robinson, James M. 1959. *A New Quest of the Historical Jesus*. London: SCM Press.
—1996. "Afterword." In Birger A. Pearson, "The Gospel According to the Jesus Semi-
    nar," 44–48. *Occasional Papers of the Institute for Antiquity and Christianity* 35.
    The Claremont Graduate School, April 1996.
—1997. "Galilean Upstarts: A Sot's Cynical Disciples?" In W. L. Petersen, J. S. Vos,
    and H. J. DeJonge, eds., *The Canonical and Non-Canonical Sayings of Jesus:
    Collected Essays in Honor of Tjitze Baarda*, 223–49. Leiden: Brill.
Saler, Benson (1993. *Conceptualizing Religion: Immanent Anthropologists, Transcen-
    dent Natives, and Unbounded Categories*. New York: Berhahn Books.
Sanders, E. P. 1985. *Jesus and Judaism*. Philadelphia: Fortress.
—1992. *Judaism: Practice and Belief 63 BCE-66 CE*. London: SCM Press.
—1993. *The Historical Figure of Jesus*. London: Penguin Books.
—2002. "Jesus, Ancient Judaism, and Modern Christianity: The Quest Continues." In
    Paula Fredriksen and Adele Reinhartz, eds., *Jesus, Judaism, and Christian Anti-
    Judaism: Reading the New Testament after the Holocaust*, 31–55. Louisville,
    KY and London: Westminster John Knox.
Sawicki, Marianne. 2000. *Crossing Galilee: Architectures of Contact in the Occupied
    Land of Jesus*. Harrisburg, PA: Trinity Press International.
Schüssler Fiorenza, Elisabeth (2000. *Jesus and the Politics of Interpretation*. New York:
    Continuum.
Schweitzer, Albert. 1954 [1906]. *The Quest of the Historical Jesus*. Trans. W. Montgomery.
    London: SCM Press.
Seeley, David. 1992. "Jesus' Death in Q." *New Testament Studies* 38: 222–34.
Simon, Nicholas. 2002. "Le Pen's Next Target?" In *The Jerusalem Report*, May 20,
    2002, http://www.jrep.com/Jewishworld/Article-16.html.
Smith, Jonathan Z. 1982a. "Introduction." In *idem*, *Imagining Religion: From Babylon
    to Jonestown*, xi–xiii. Chicago: University of Chicago Press.
—1982b. "Fences and Neighbors: Some Contours of Early Judaism." In *idem*,
    Imagining Religion: From Babylon to Jonestown, 1–18. Chicago: University of
    Chicago Press.
—1990. *Drudgery Divine: On the Comparison of Early Christianities and the Religions
    of Late Antiquity*. Chicago: University of Chicago Press.
Stark, Rodney. 1996. *The Rise of Christianity: A Sociologist Reconsiders History*.
    Princeton, NJ: Princeton University Press.

Tannehill, Robert C. 1981. "The Pronouncement Story and Its Types." *Semeia* 20: 1–14.

Tuckett, C. M. 1989. "A Cynic Q?" *Biblica* 70: 349–76.

Vaage, Leif E. 1988. "The Woes in Q (and Matthew and Luke): Deciphering the Rhetoric of Criticism." In David J. Lull, ed., *Society of Biblical Literature 1988 Seminar Papers*, 582–607. Atlanta: Scholars Press.

—1994. *Galilean Upstarts: Jesus' First Followers According to Q.* Valley Forge, PA: Trinity Press International.

Vermès, Geza. 1973. *Jesus the Jew: A Historian's Reading of the Gospels.* Philadelphia: Fortress.

—1993. *The Religion of Jesus the Jew.* Philadelphia: Fortress.

Wright, N. T. 1992. *The New Testament and the People of God.* Minneapolis: Fortress.

—1993. "Taking the Text with Her Pleasure: A Post-Post-Modernist Response to J. Dominic Crossan, *The Historical Jesus: The Life of a Mediterranean Jewish Peasant.*" *Theology* 96: 303–9.

Index of Subjects

Index of Names

Index of Ancient Texts